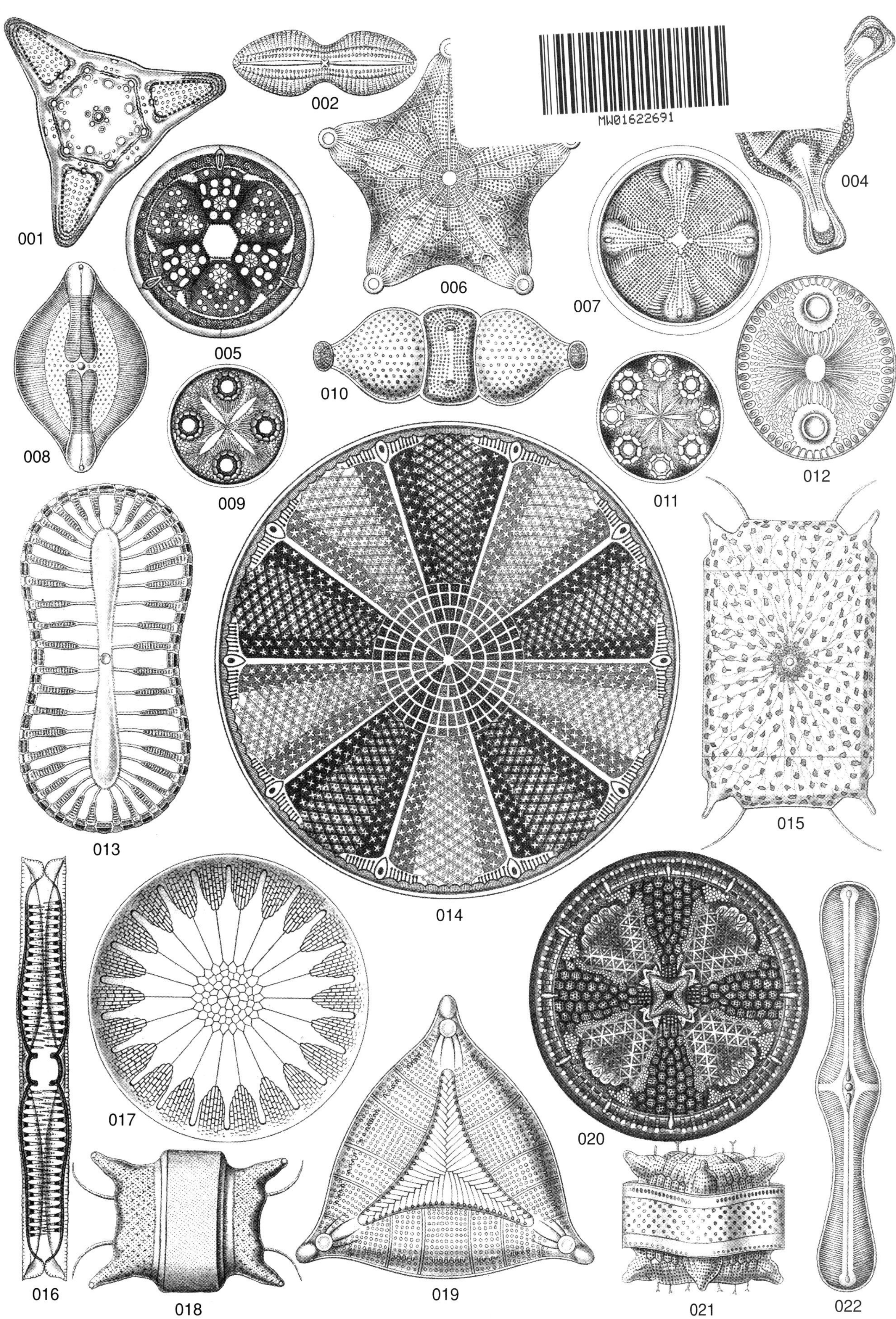



Various species of diatoms (a type of unicellular plant).

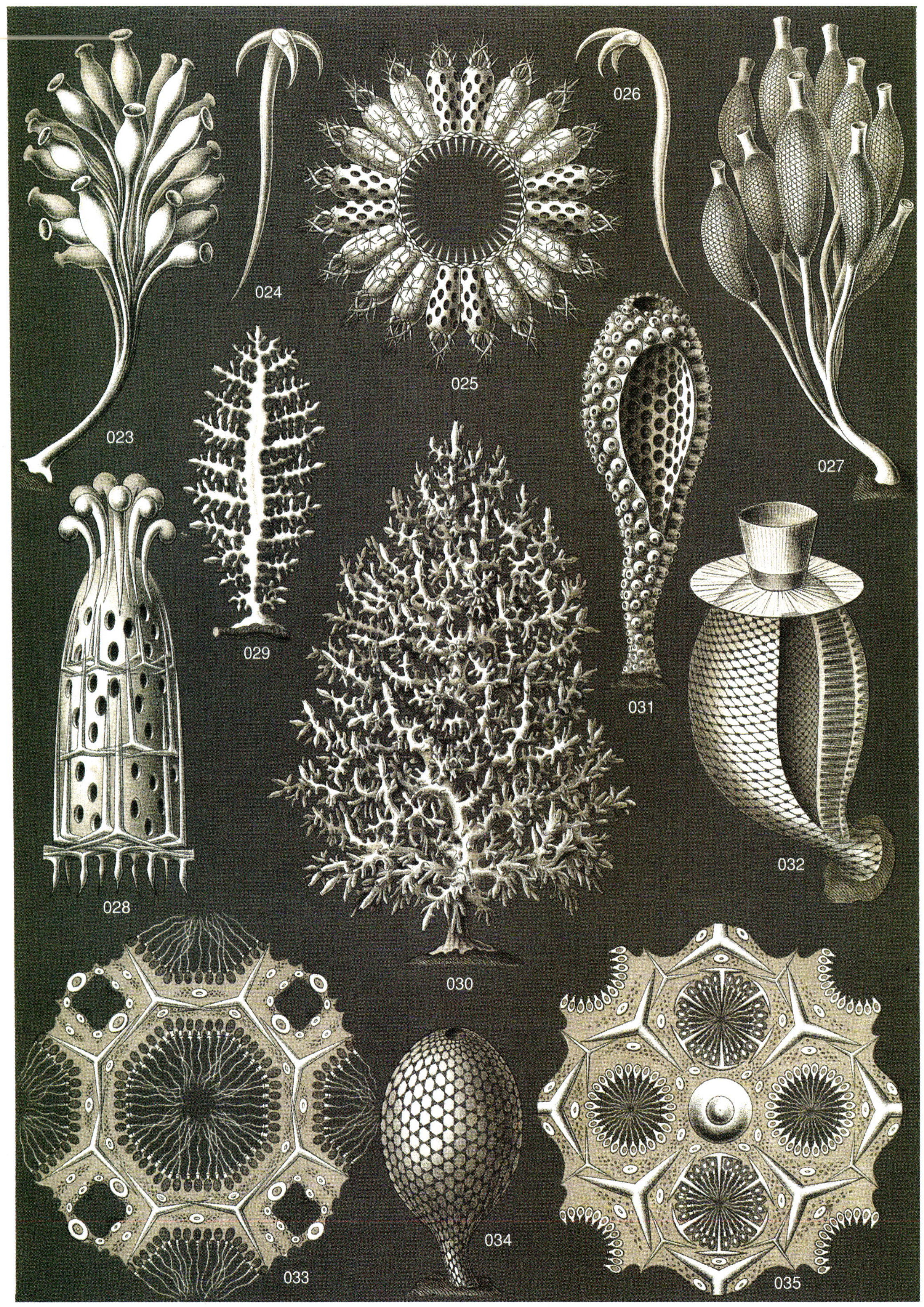




Various species of calcareous sponges.

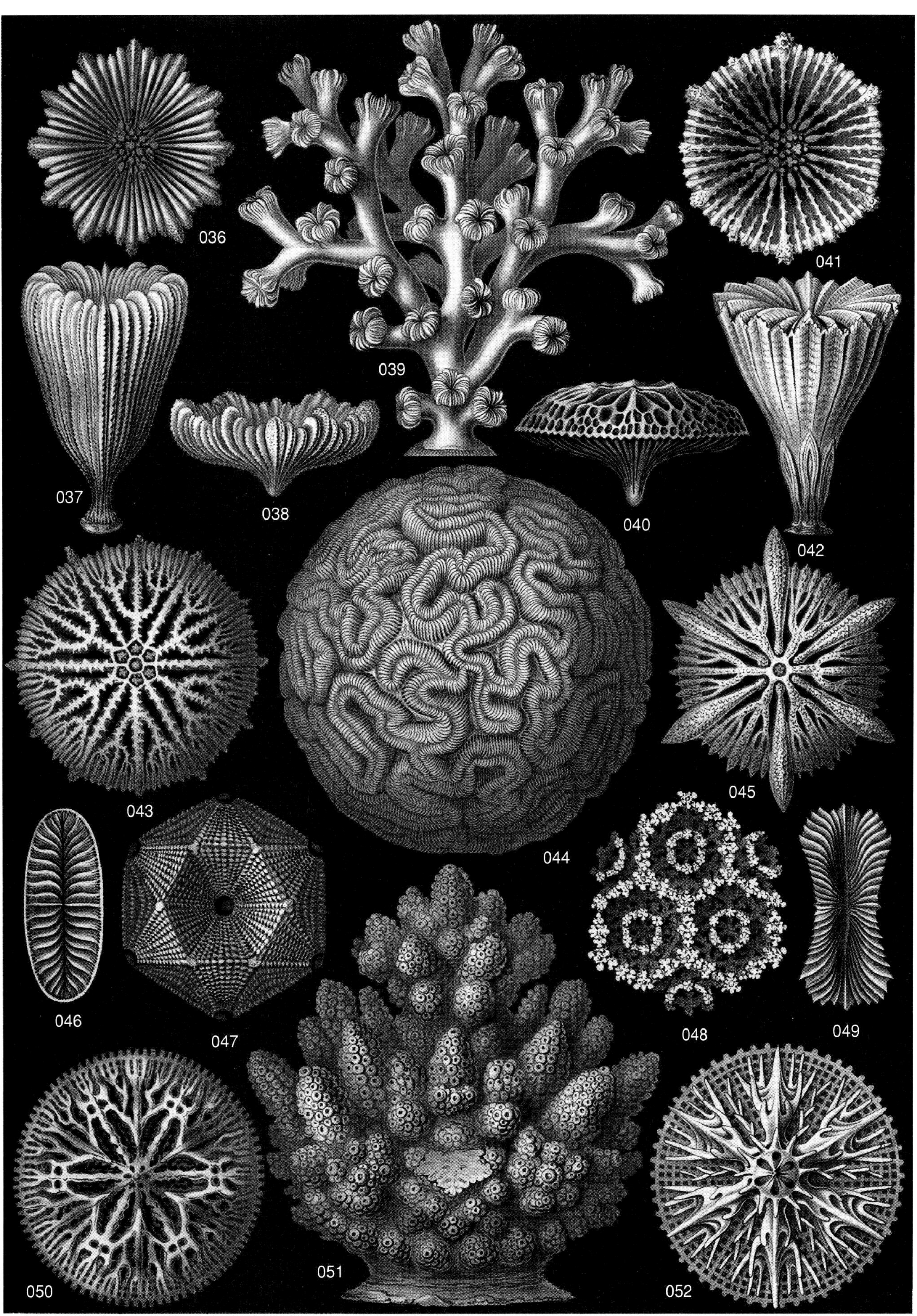


Various species of star corals.

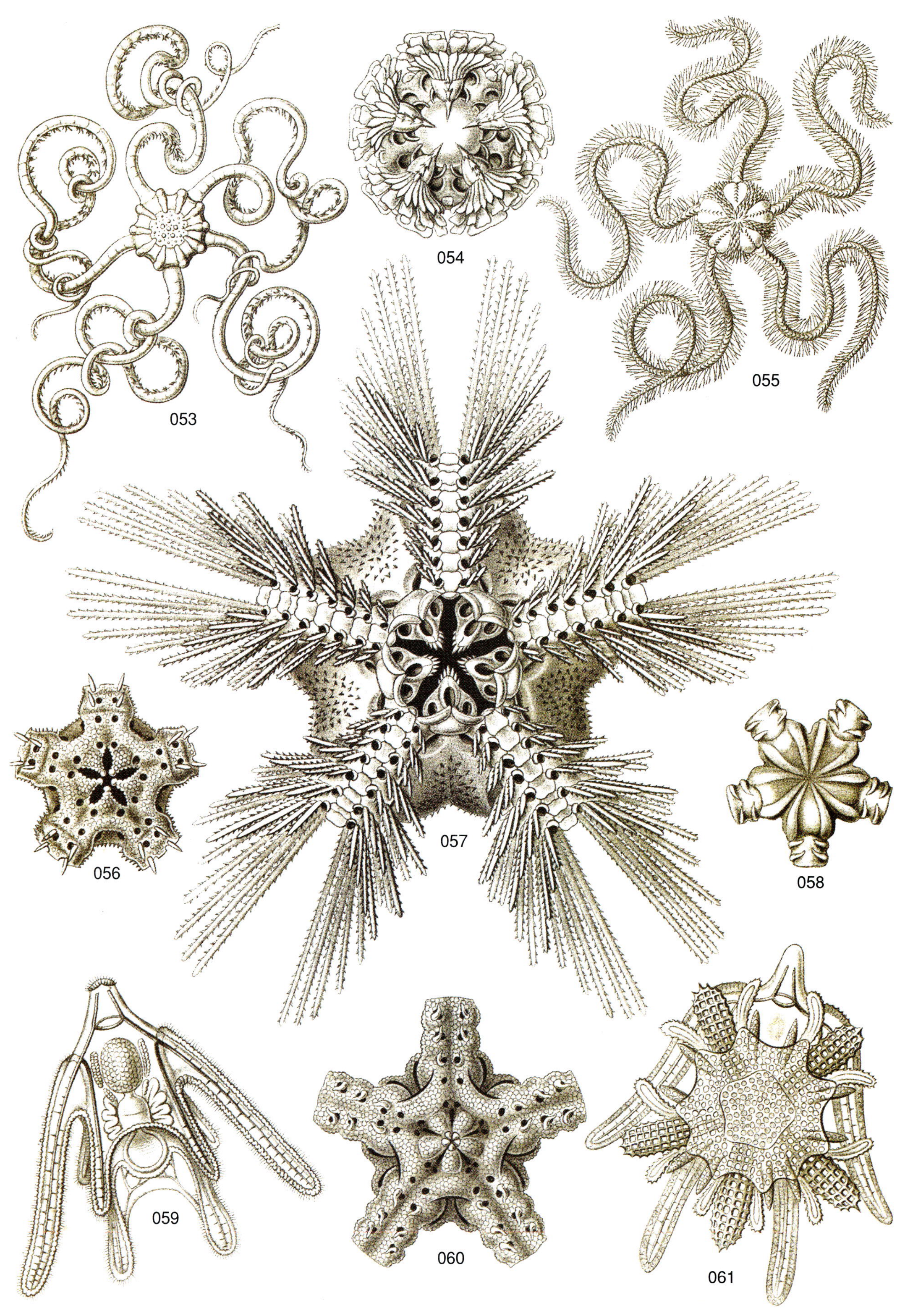




Various types of starfishes.

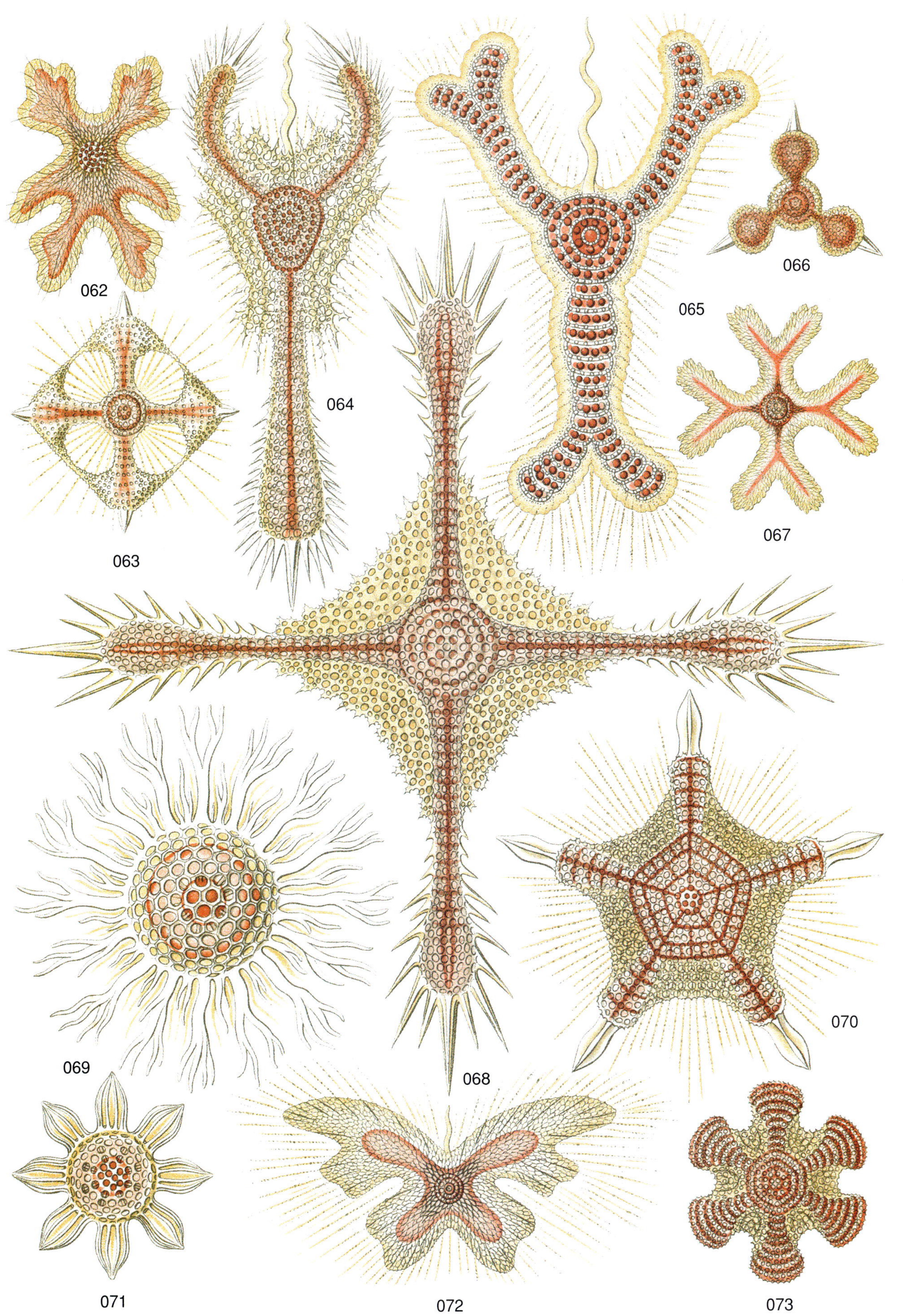


Various species of Radiolaria (a type of marine Protozoa).

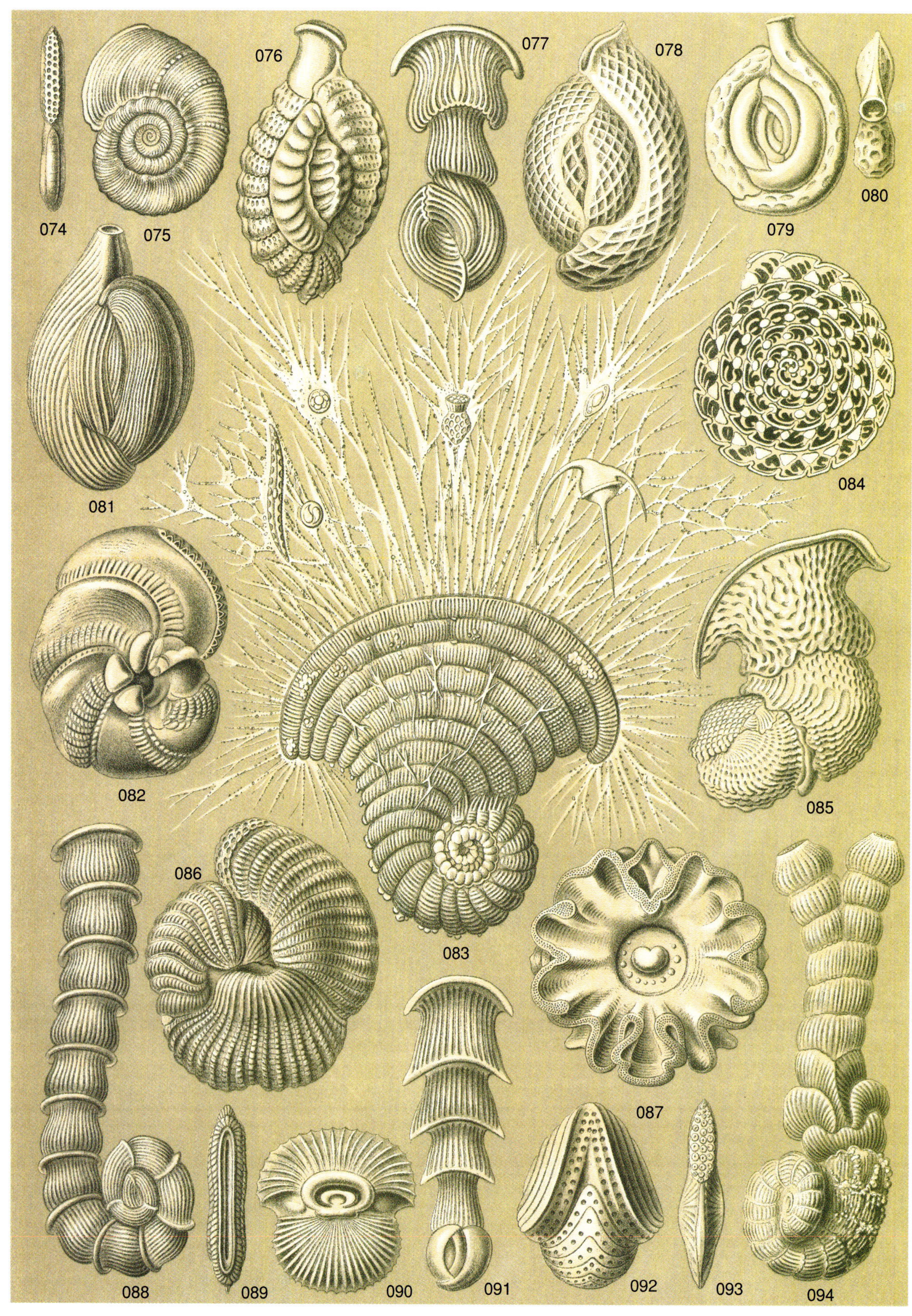




Various species of Protozoa related to the Foraminifera.

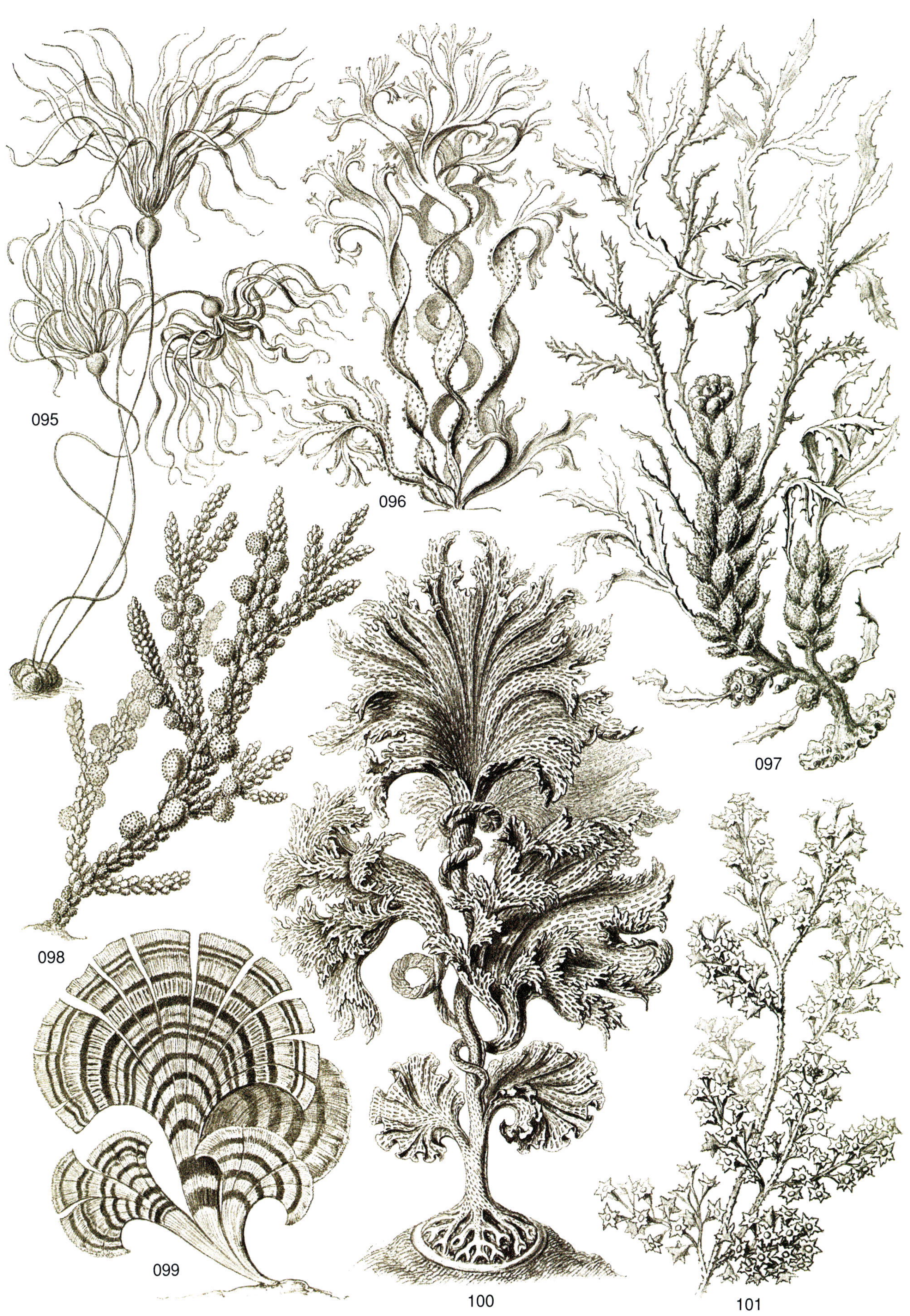


Various species of brown seaweed (algae).

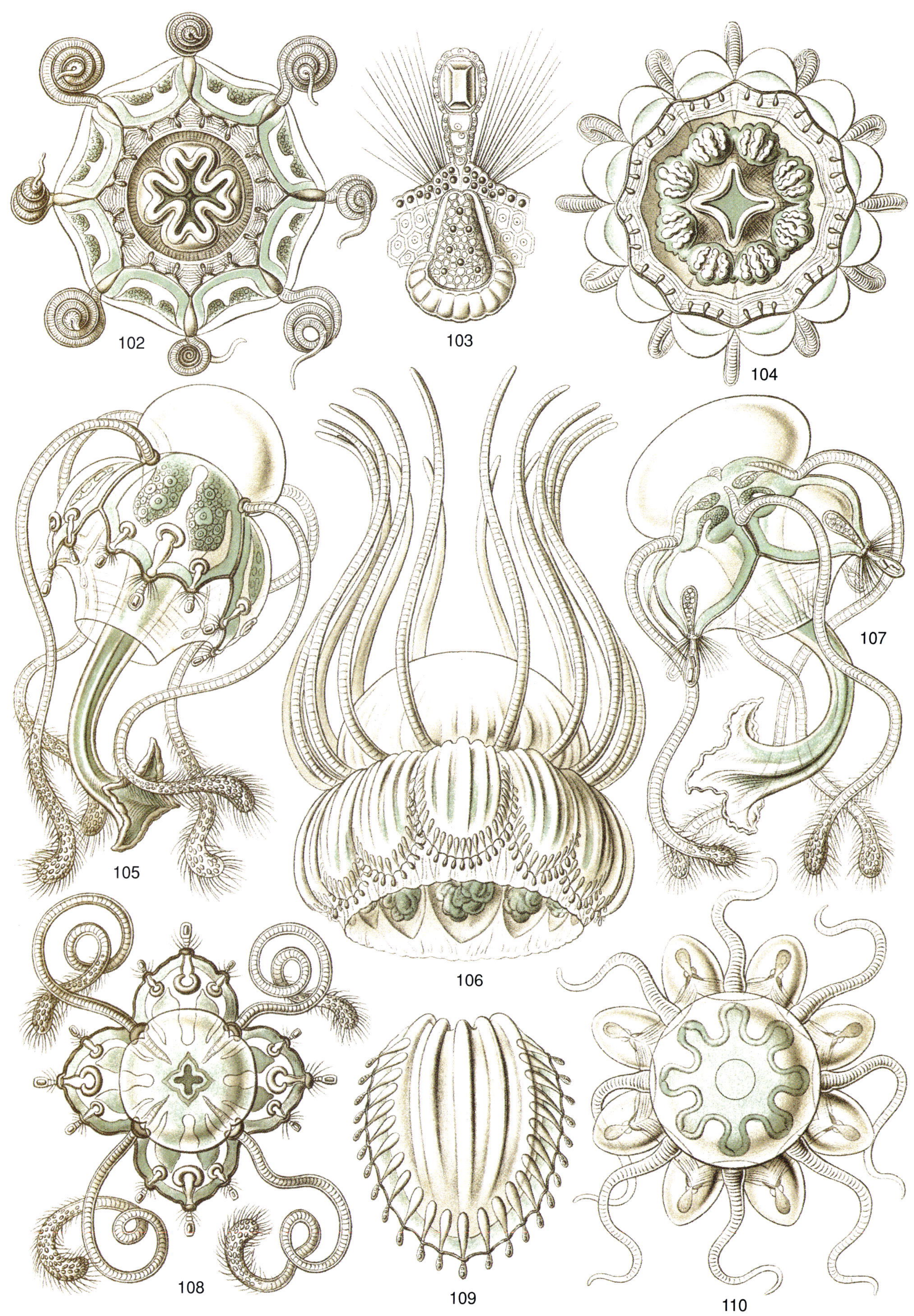




Various species of Narcomedusae (in the same class as hydras).

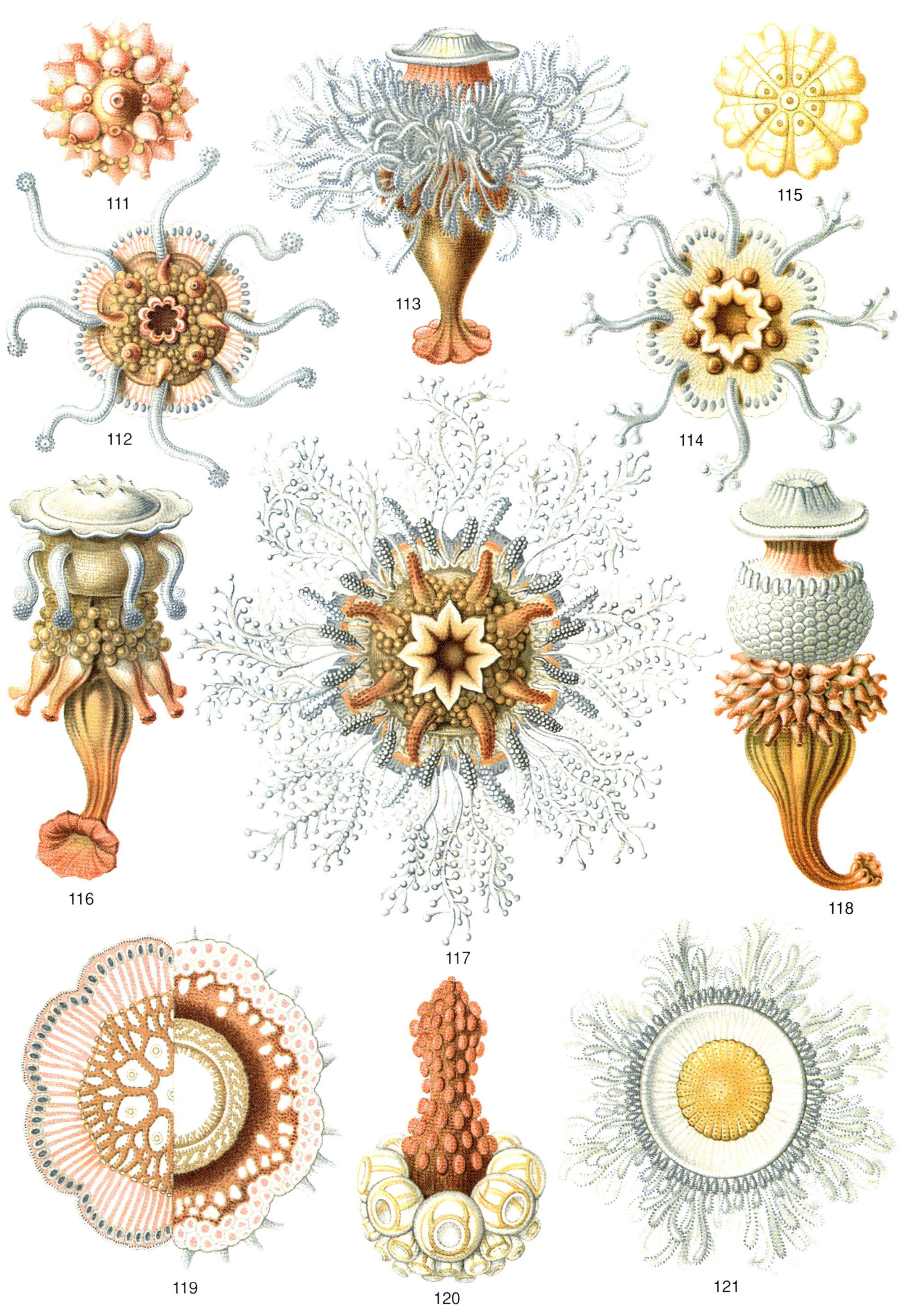


Various species of Siphonophora (in the same class as hydras).

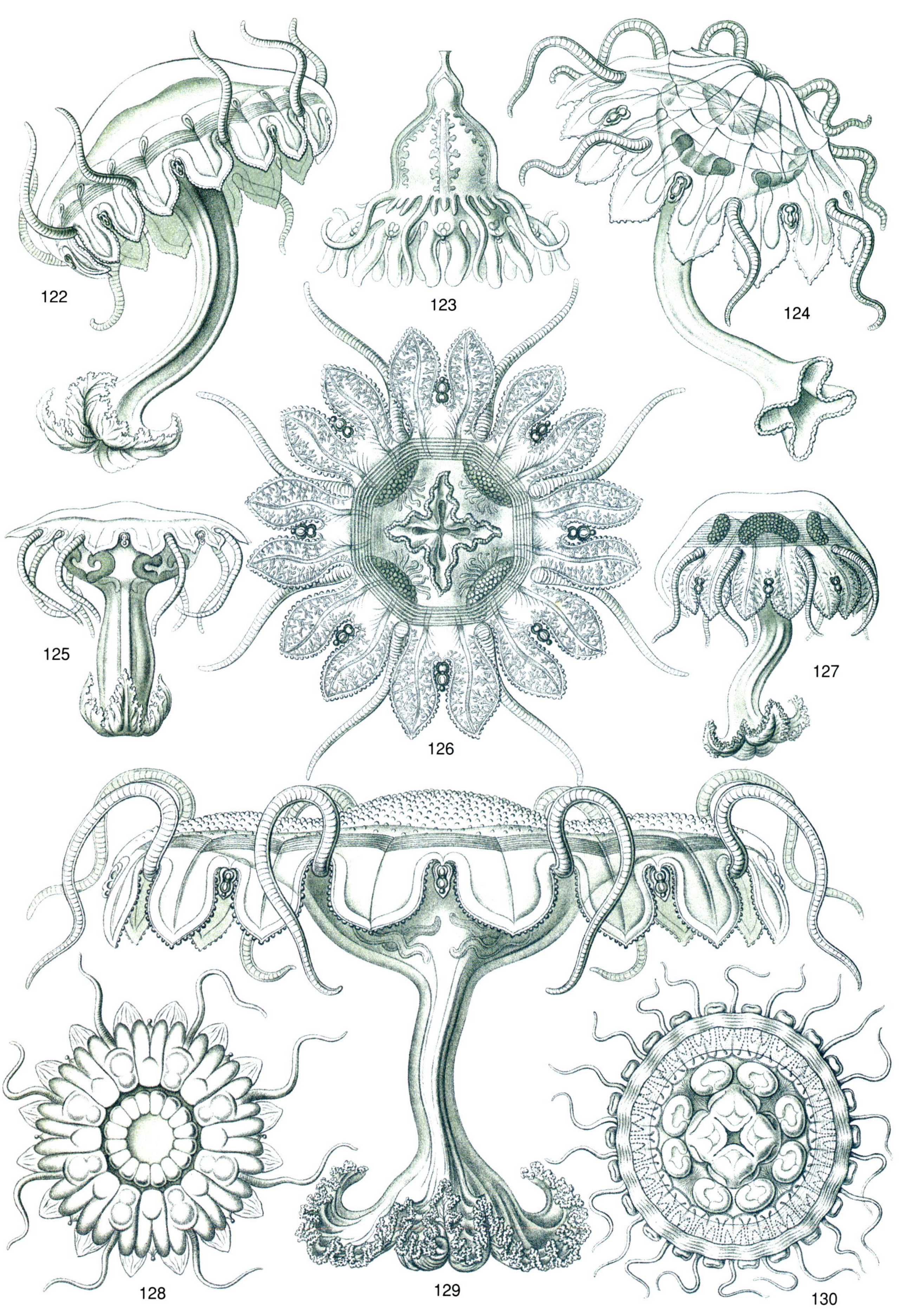


Various species of jellyfishes.

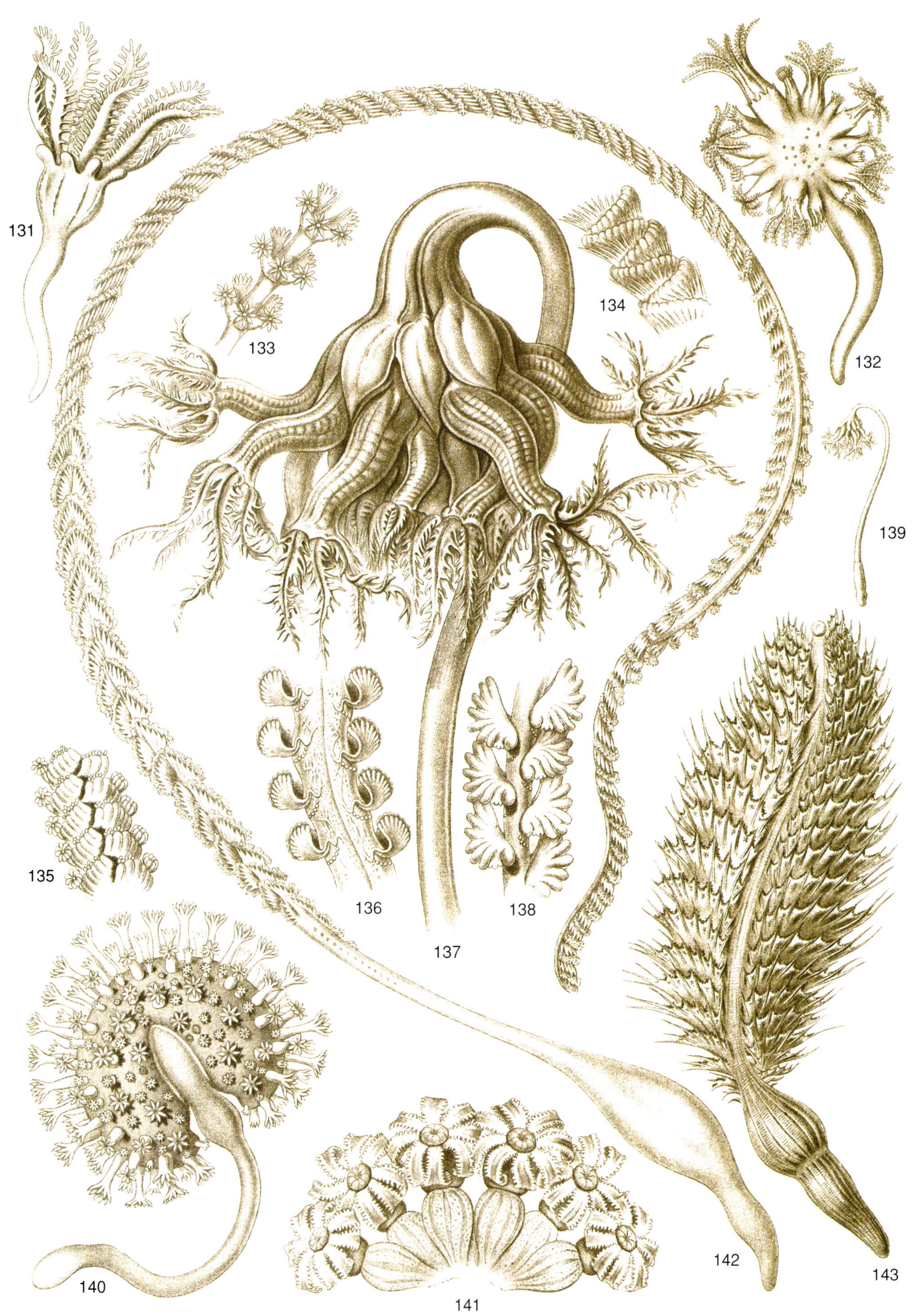


Various species of Pennatulacea (sea pens, a type of soft coral).

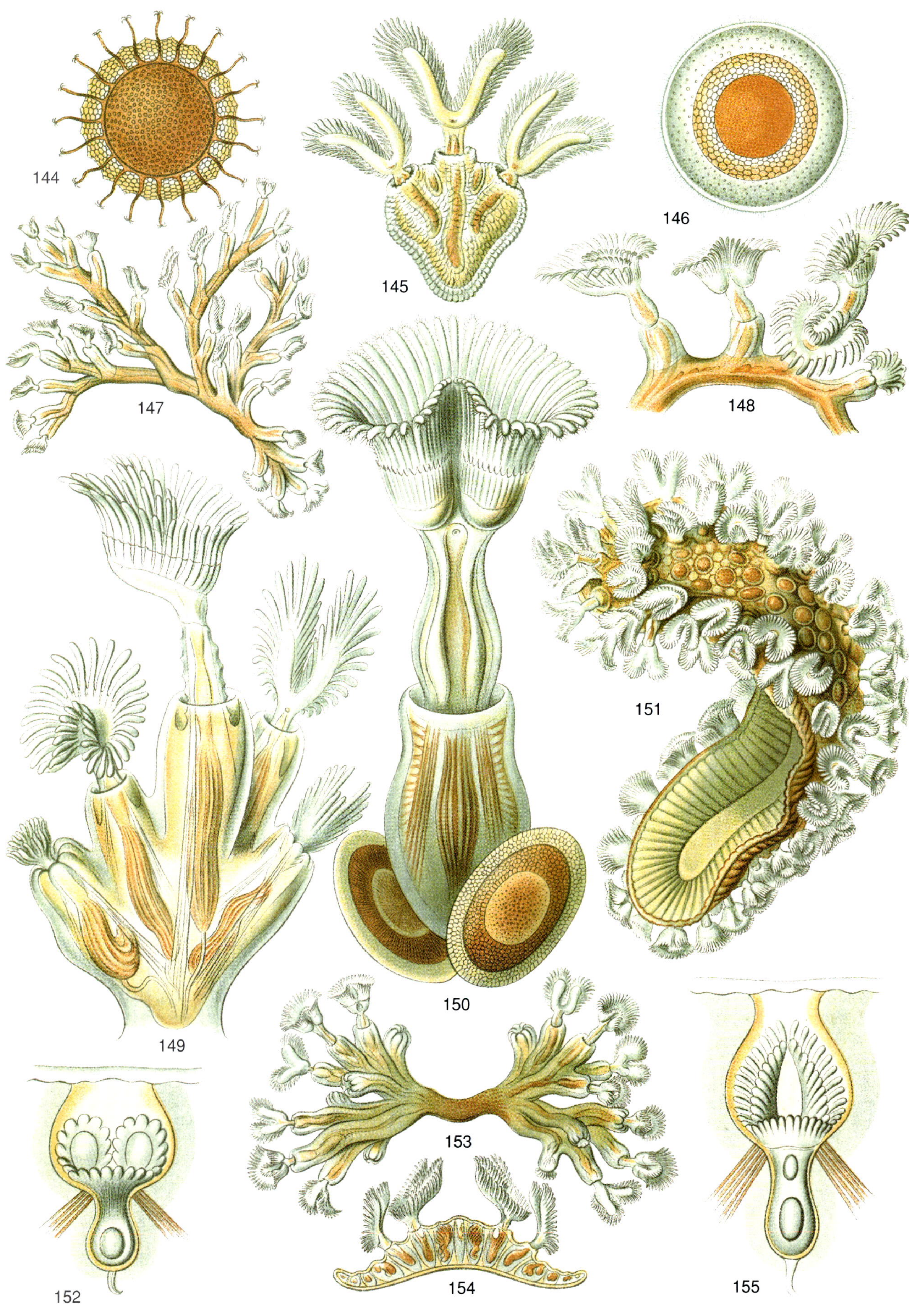




Various species of moss animals (marine animals living in colonies).

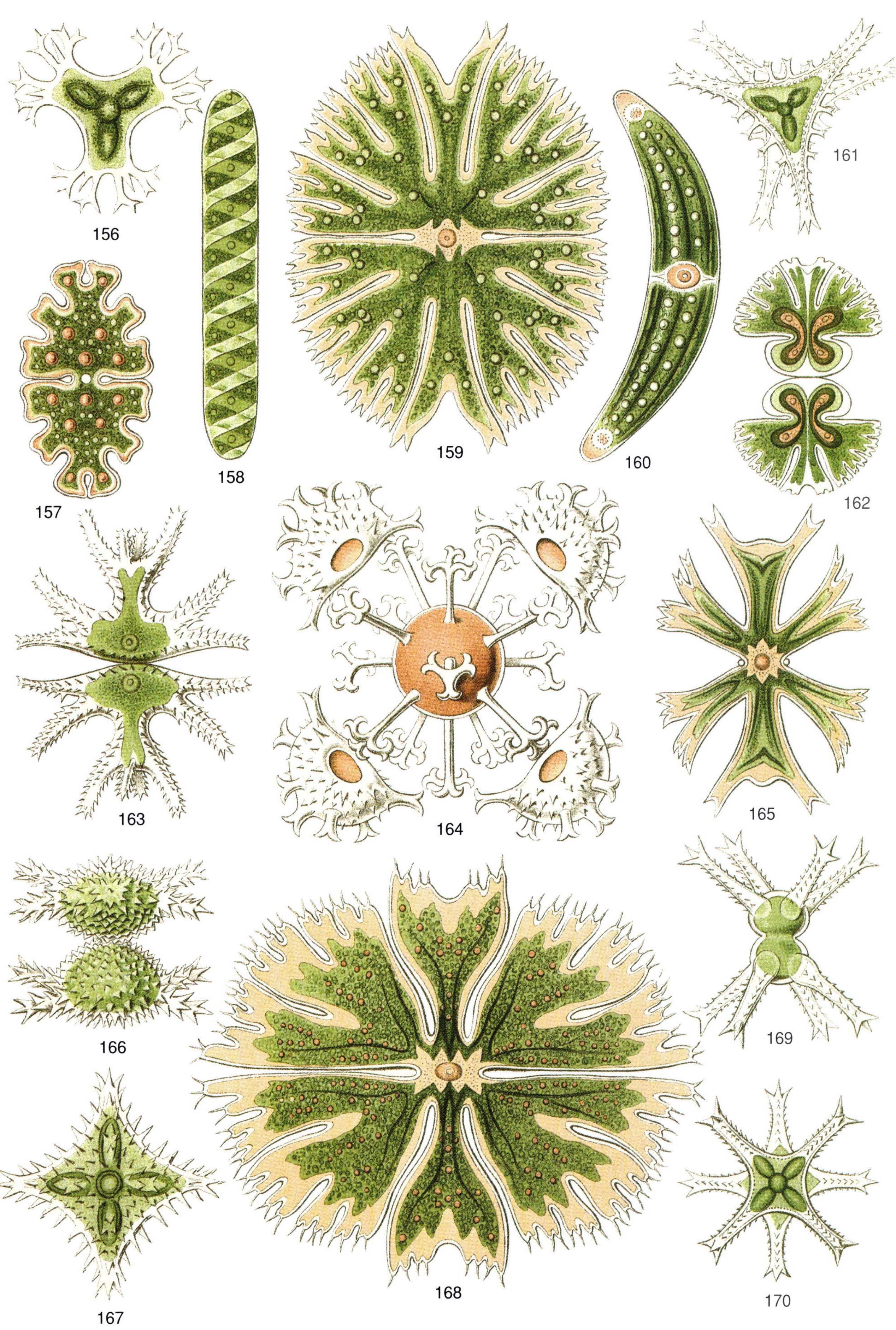


Various species of Desmidiaceae (a type of unicellular algae).

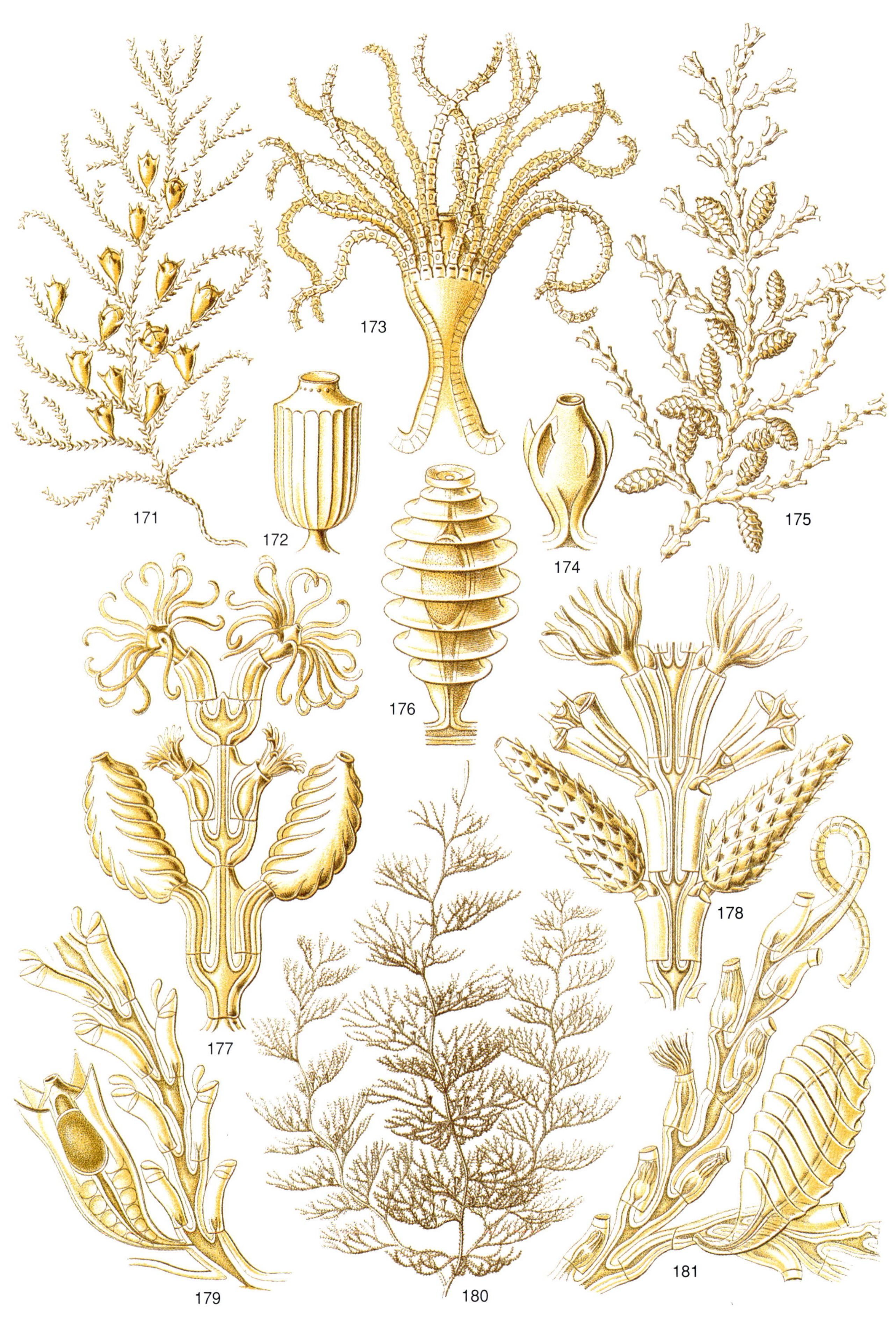


 Various species of Sertulariidae (a family of hydroid polyps).

Various species of Trachymedusae (related to hydras).

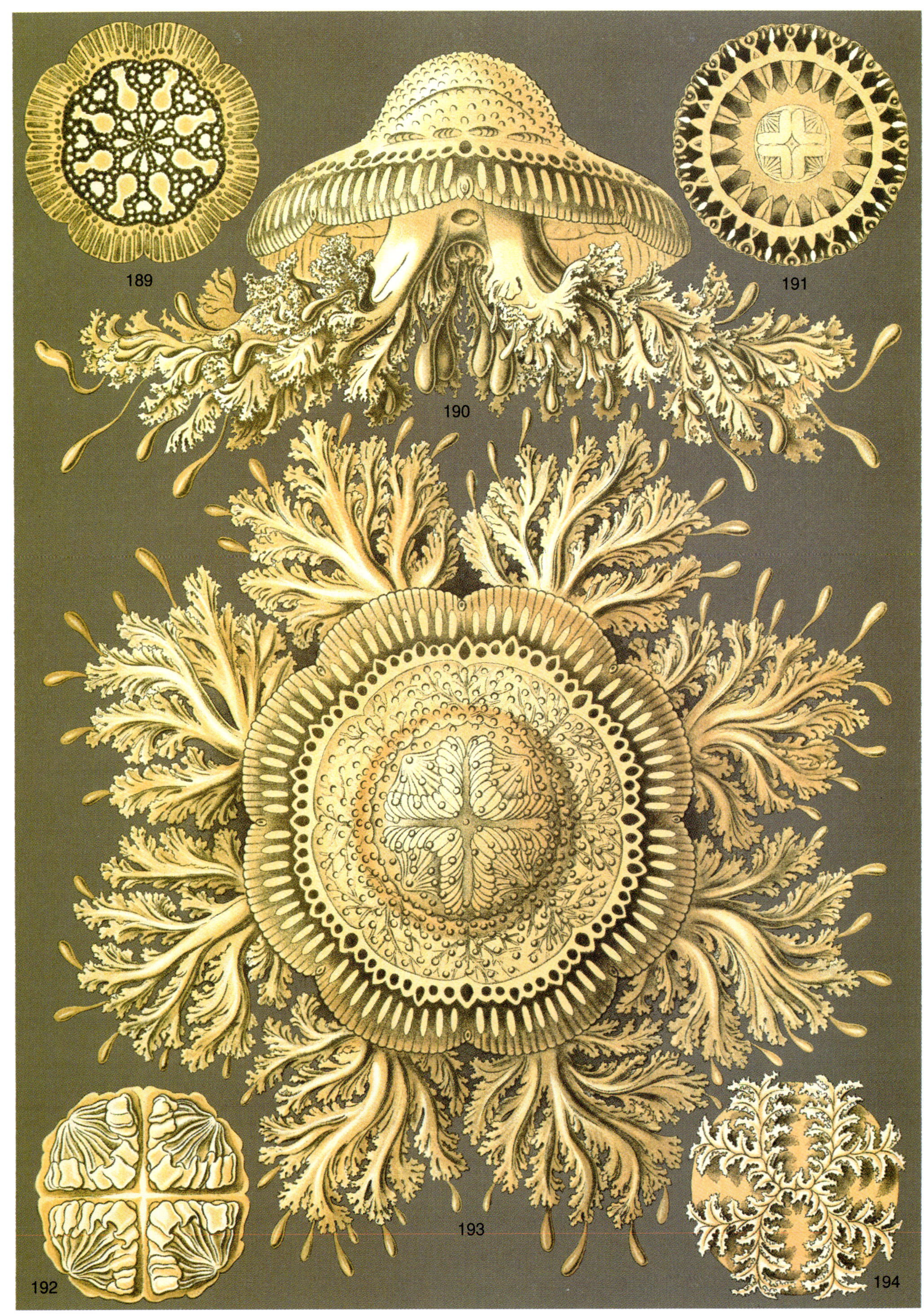




Various species of Rhizostomeae (an order of jellyfishes).

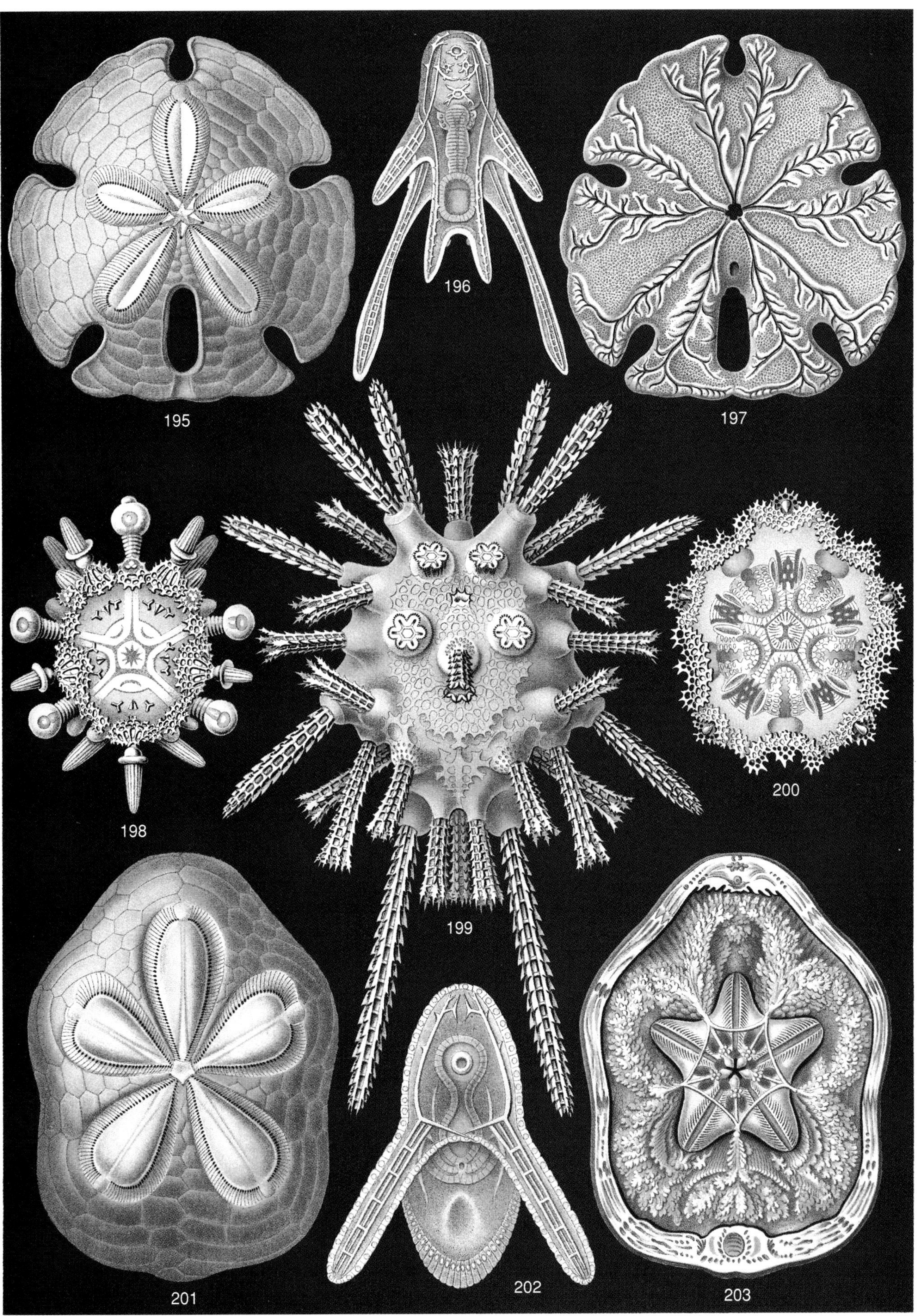


Various species of sea-urchins.

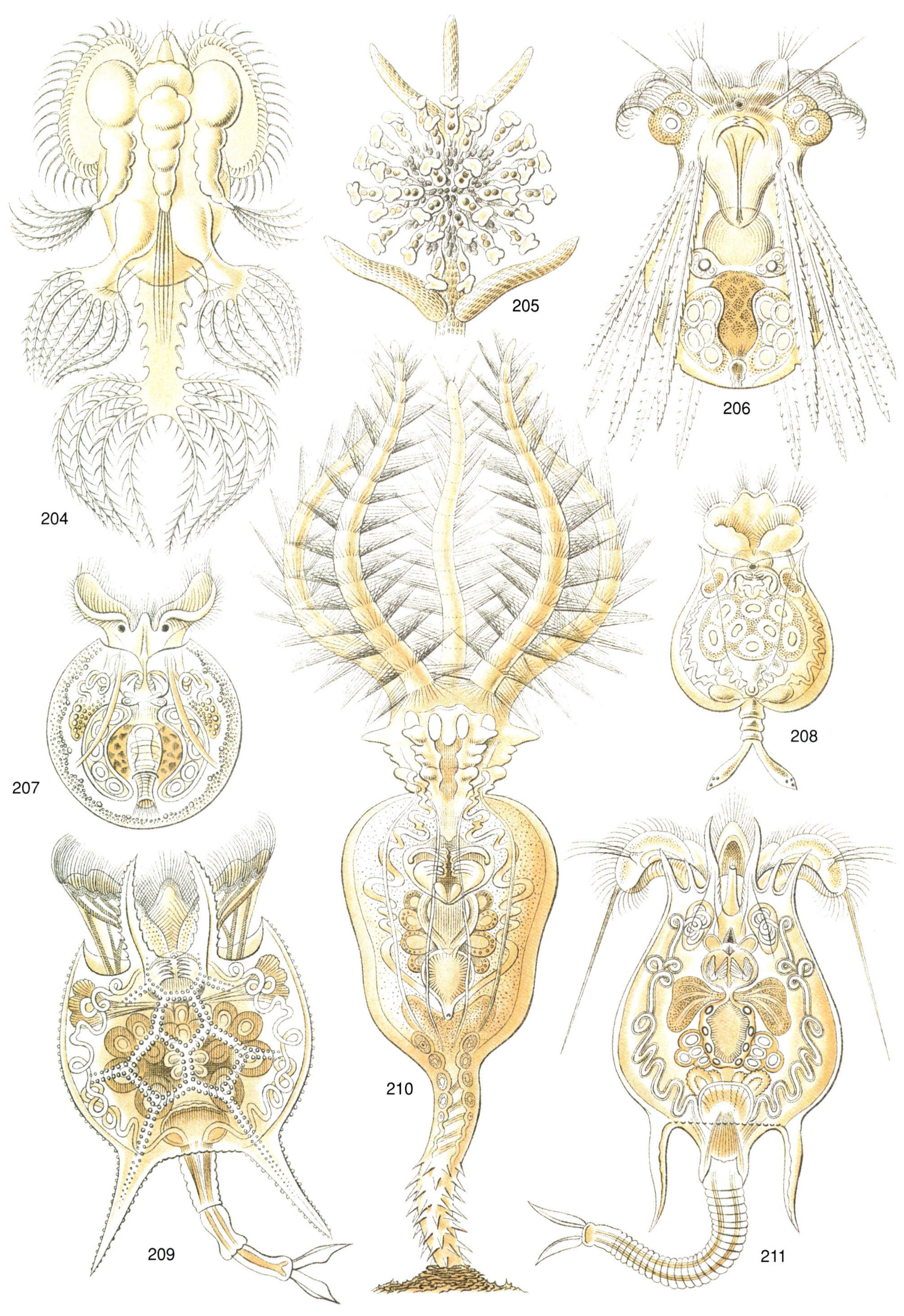




Various species of rotifers (a class of animals related to roundworms).

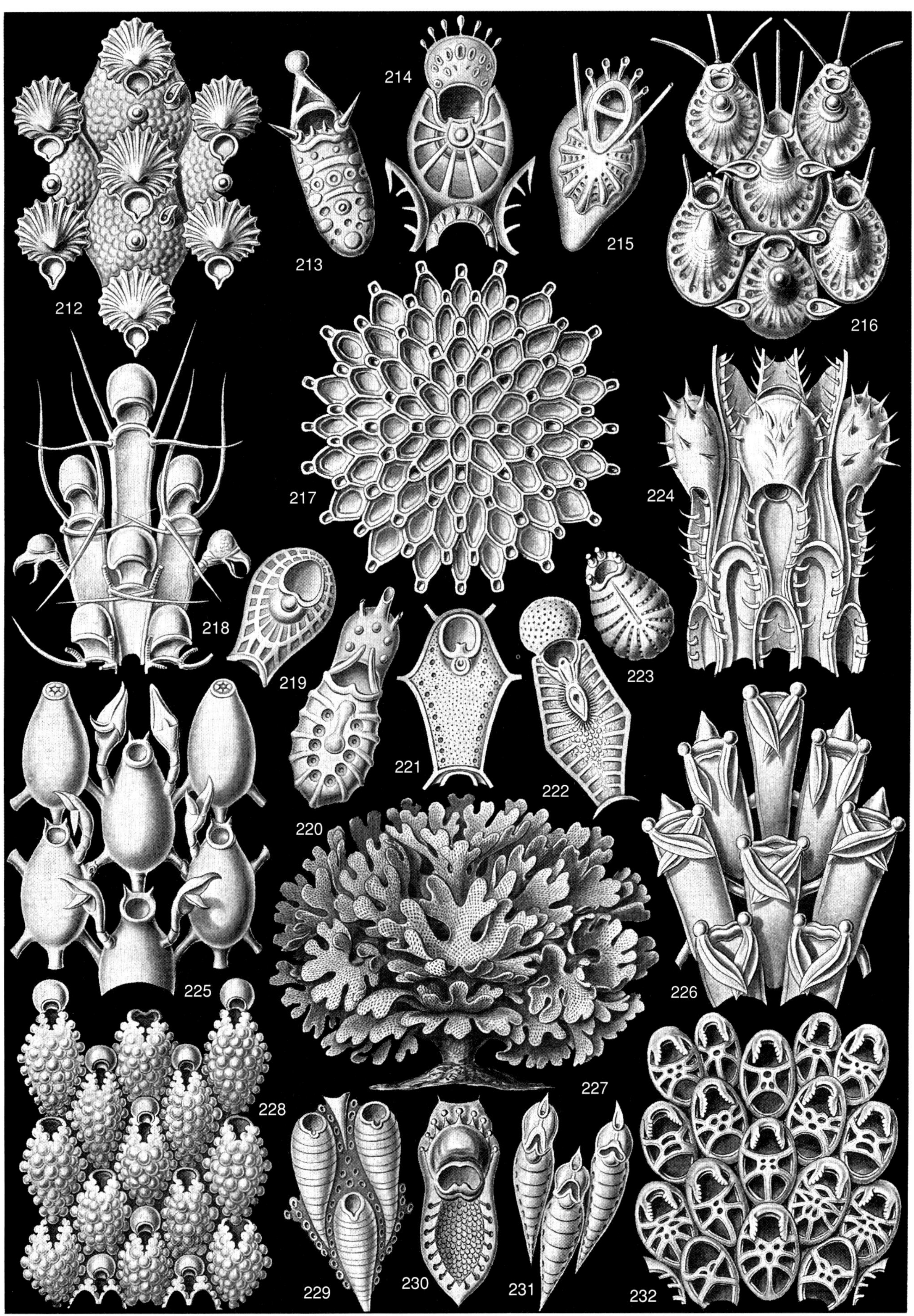


Various species of moss animals (marine animals living in colonies).

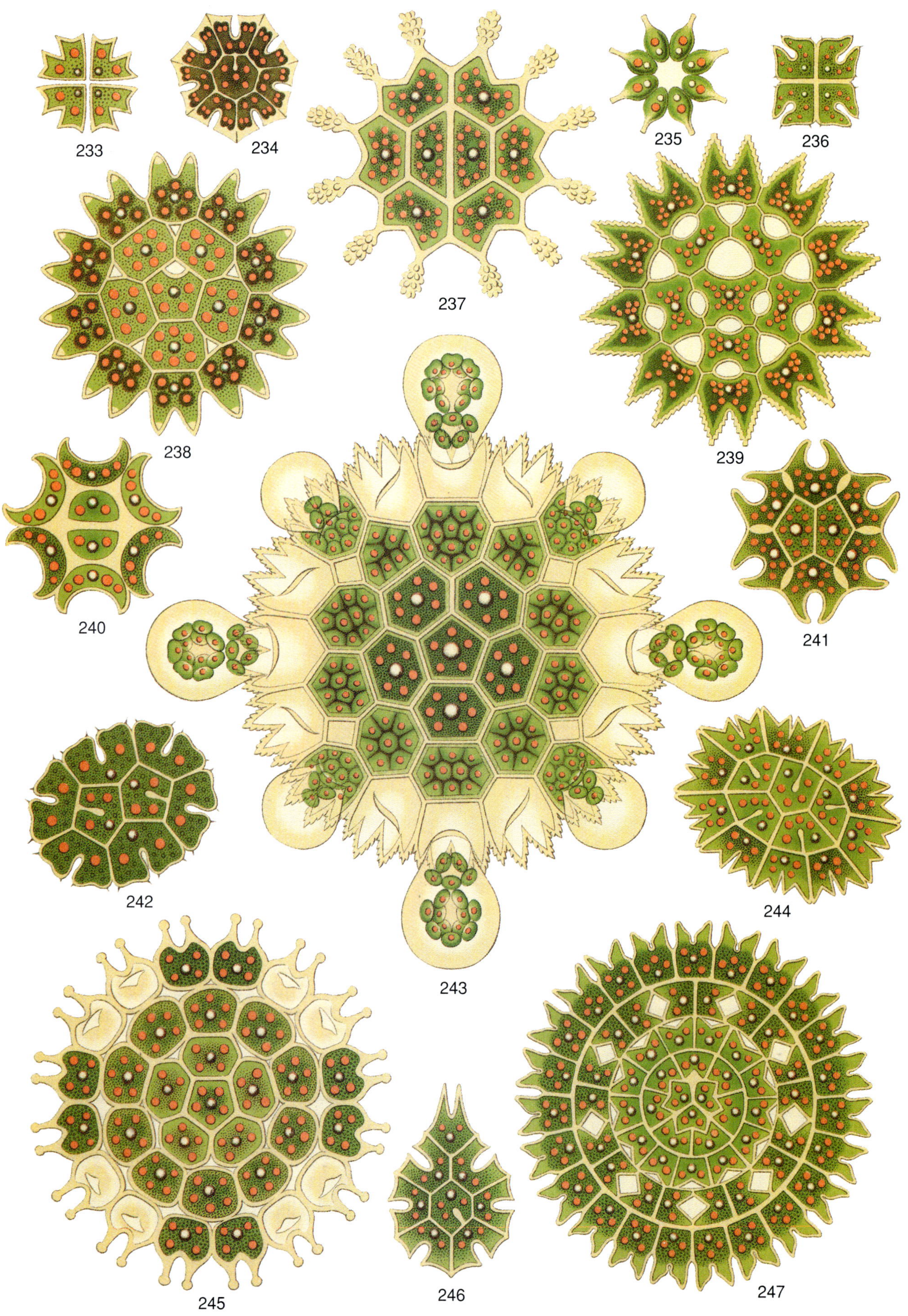




Various species of Hydrodictyaceae (colonial algae).

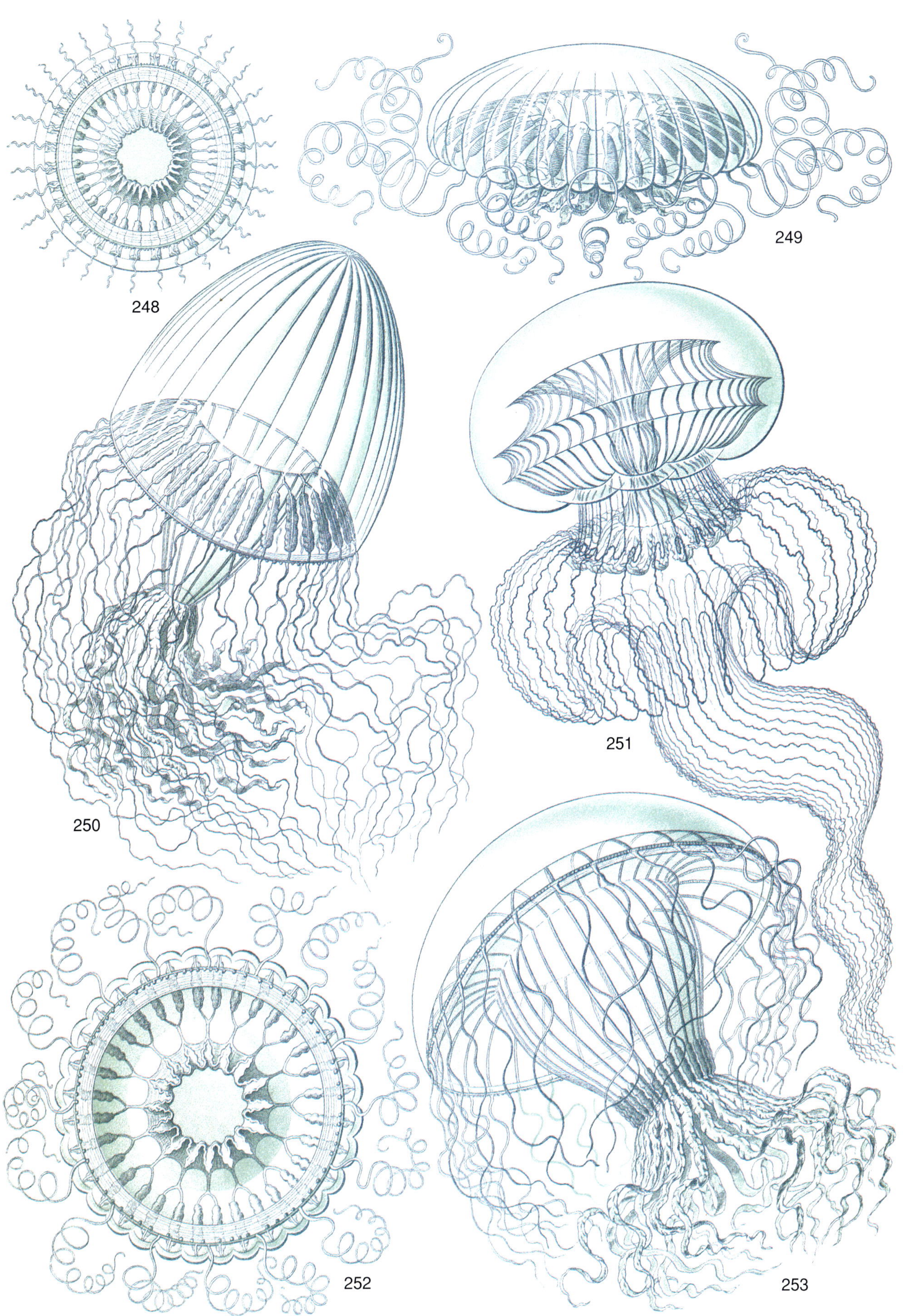


Various types of Leptomedusae (related to hydras).

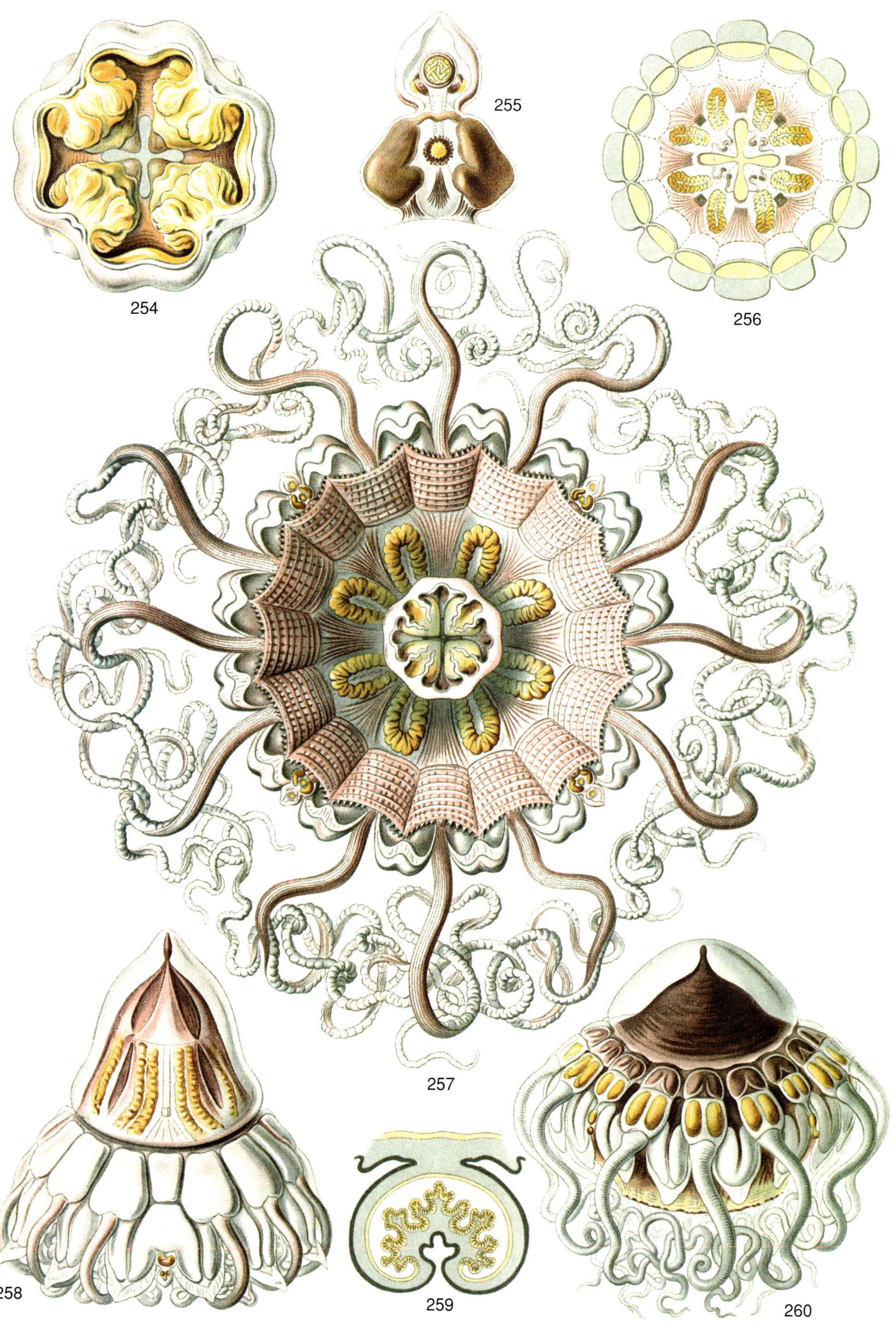




Various species of Periphylla (a genus of jellyfishes).

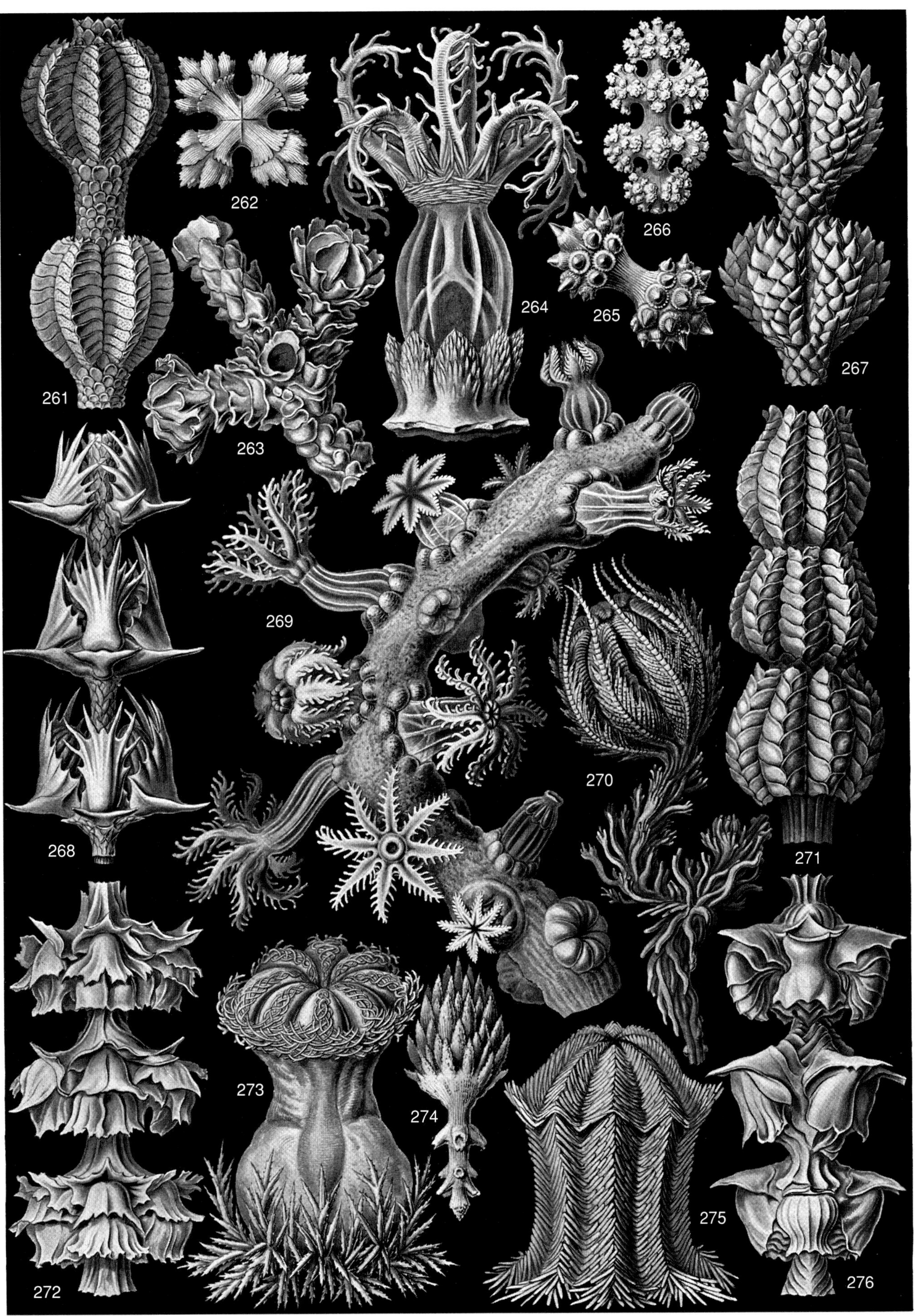


Various species of horny corals.

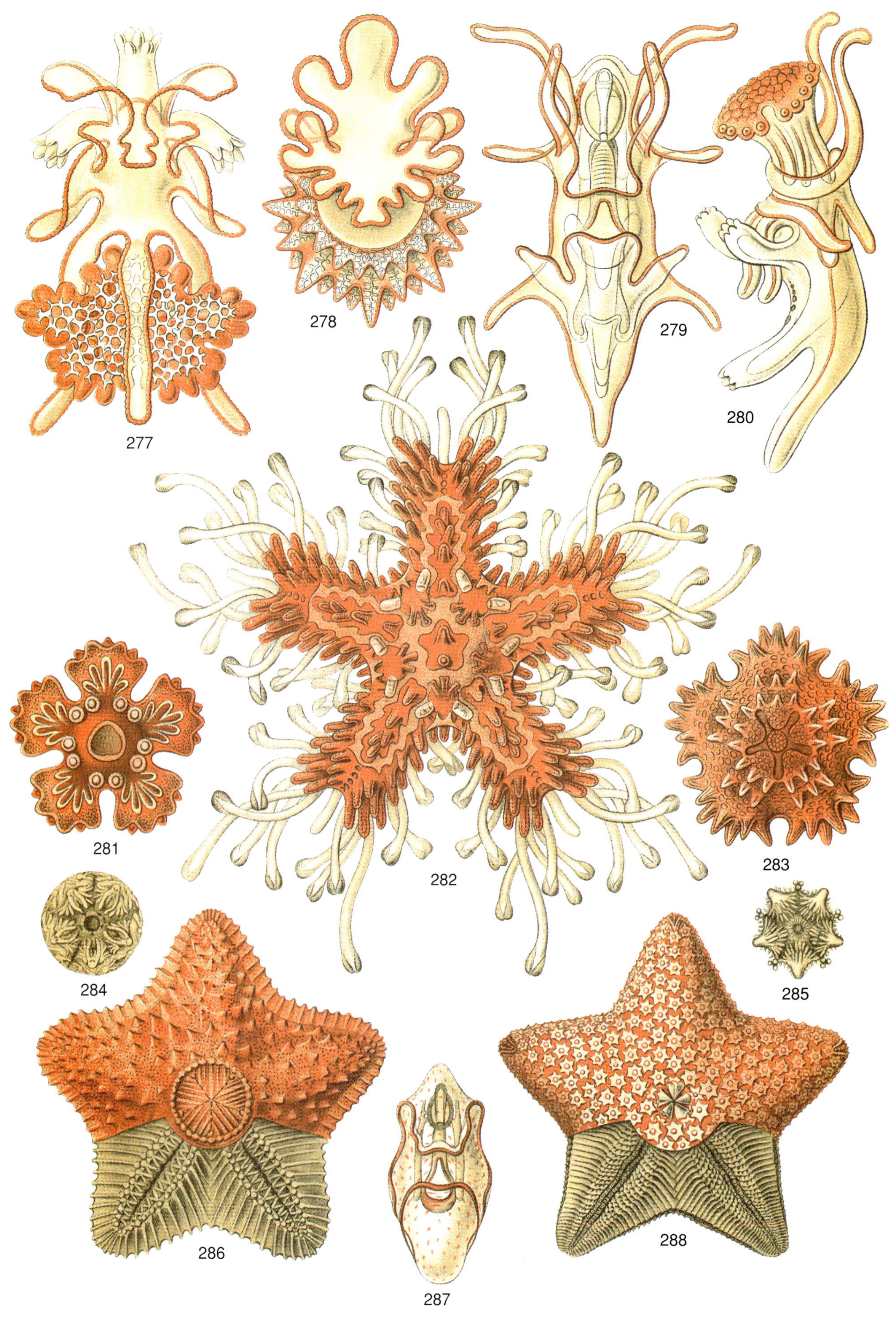




Various species of starfishes.

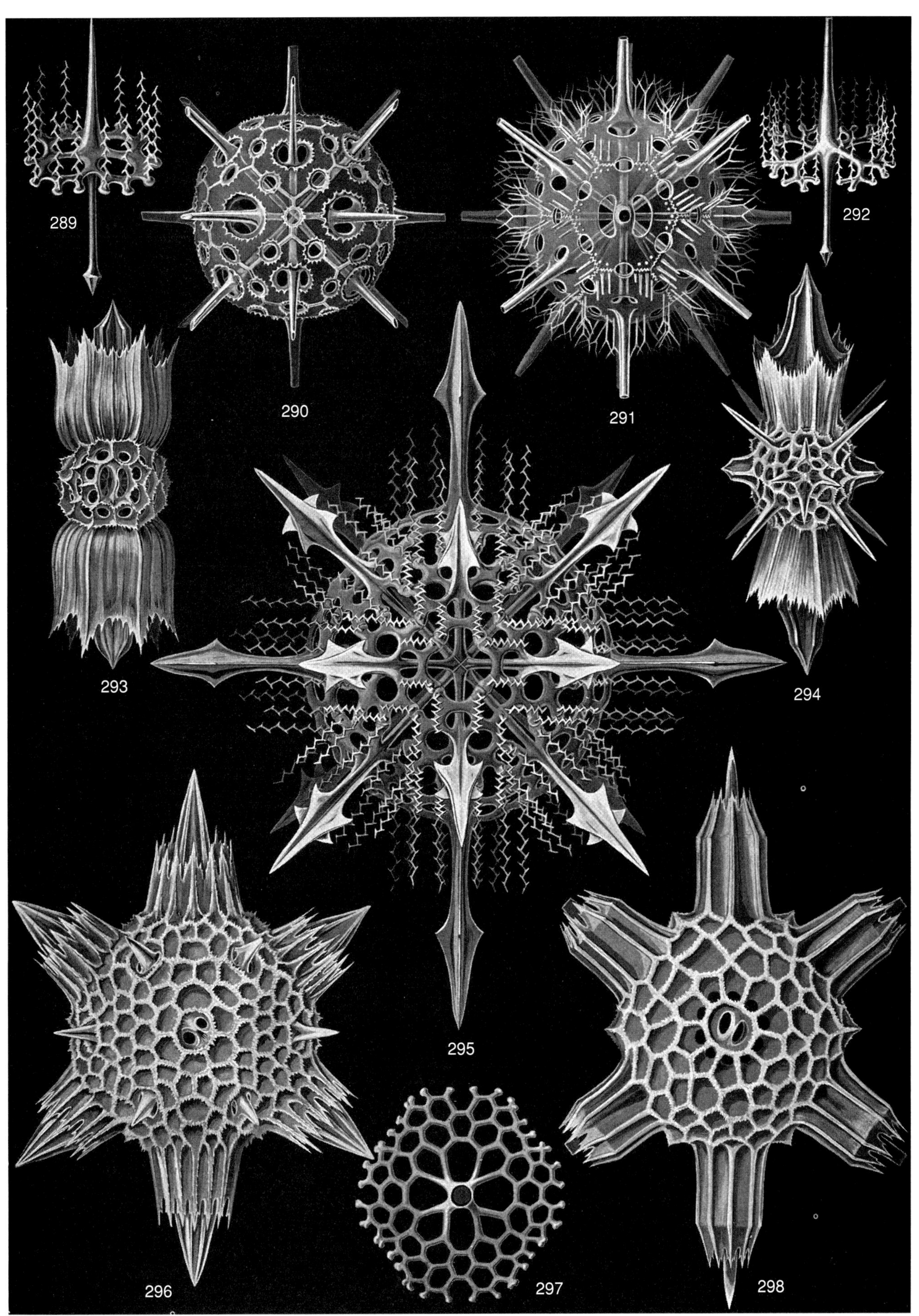


Various species of Radiolaria (a type of marine Protozoa).

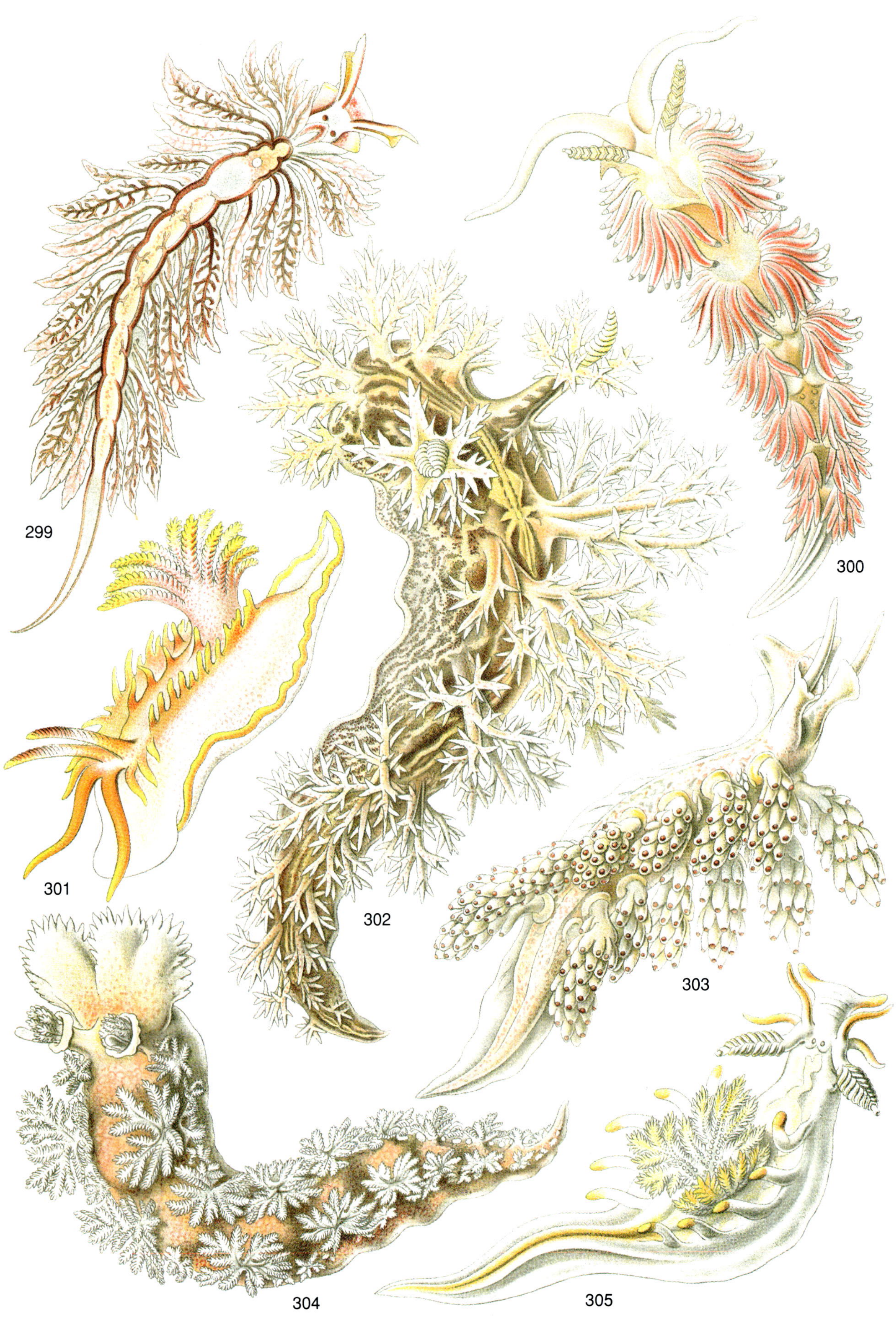




Various species of true sea slugs (Nudibranchia).

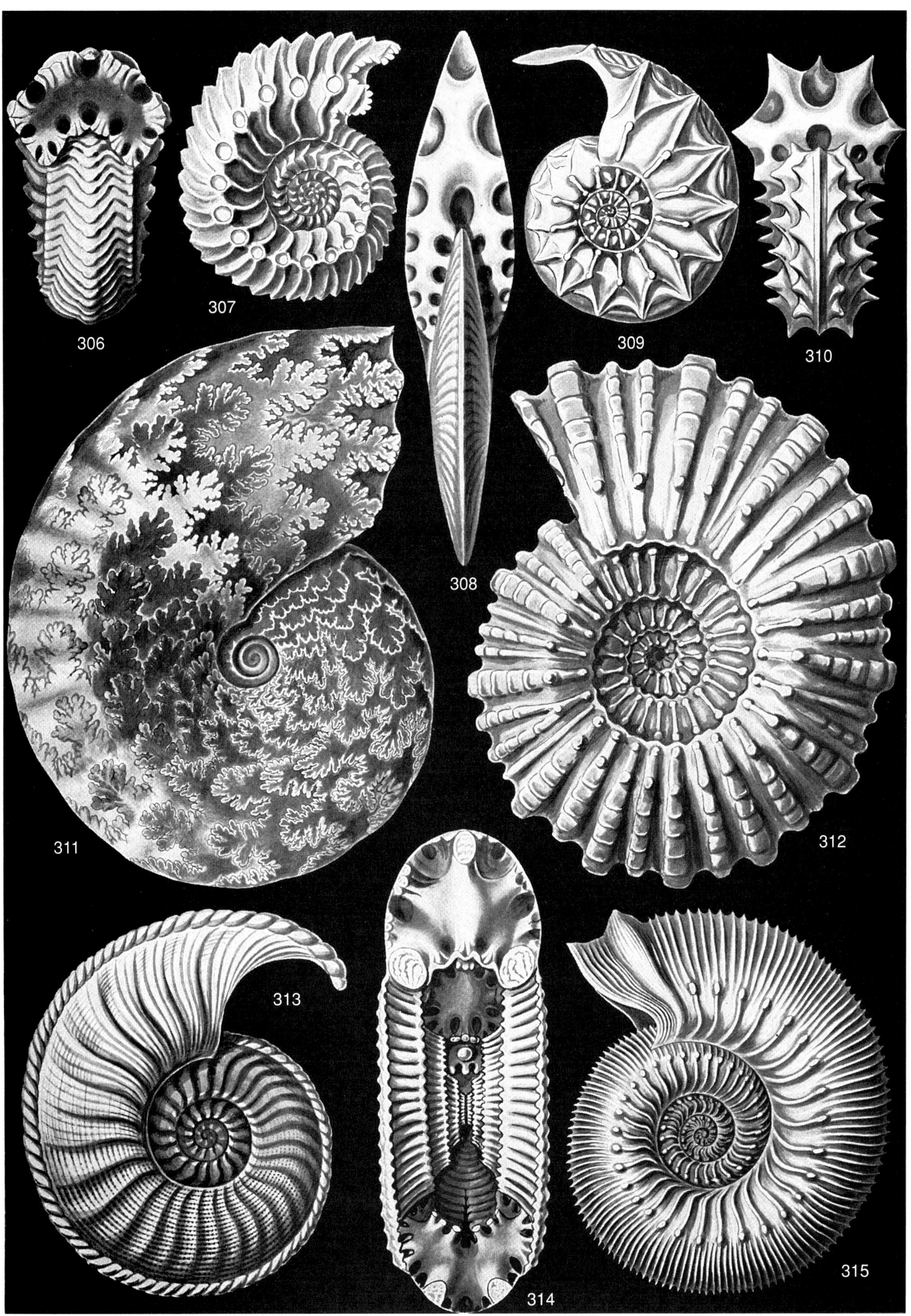


Shells of various ammonites (extinct cephalopods).

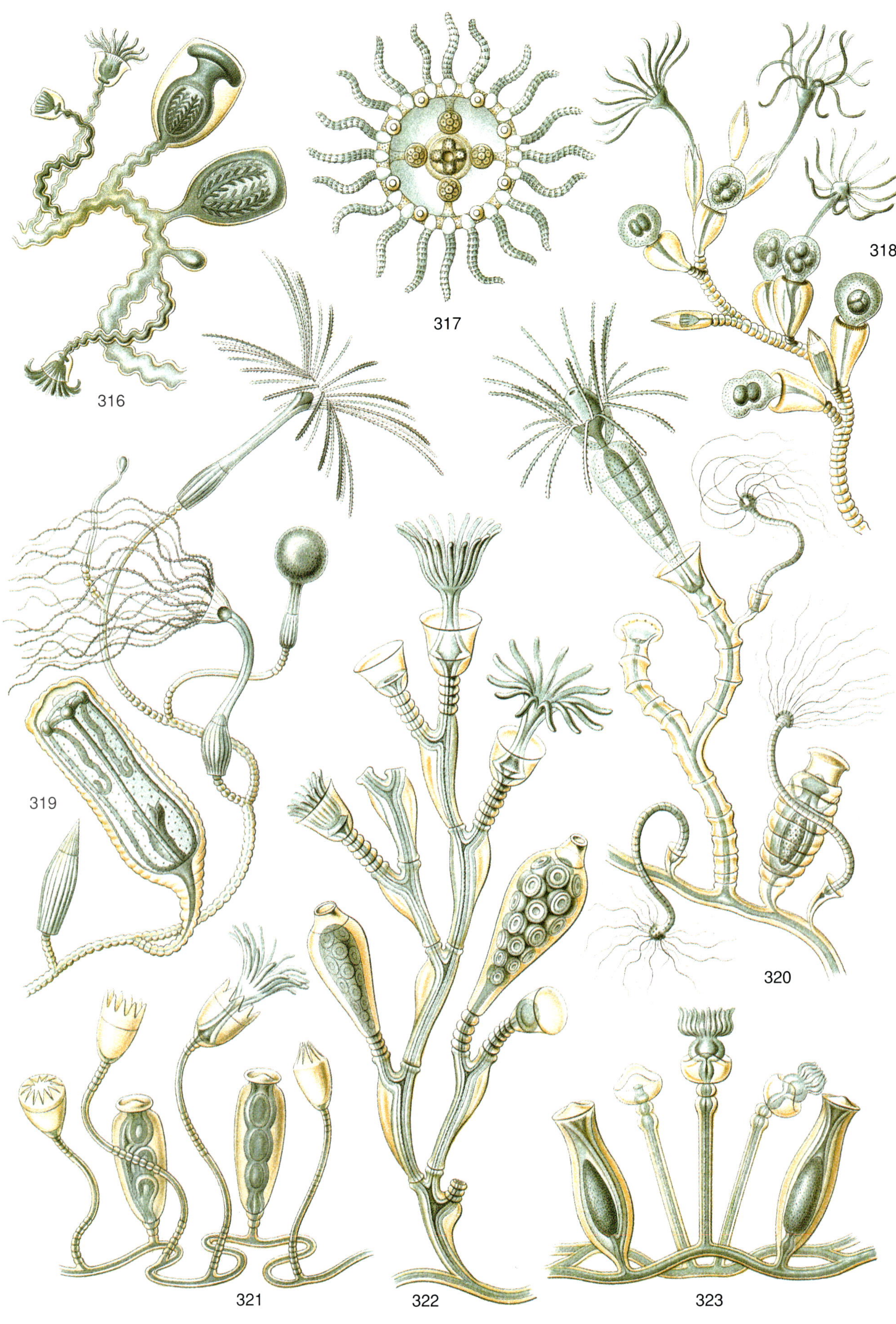




Various species of Campanulariidae (a family of hydroid polyps).

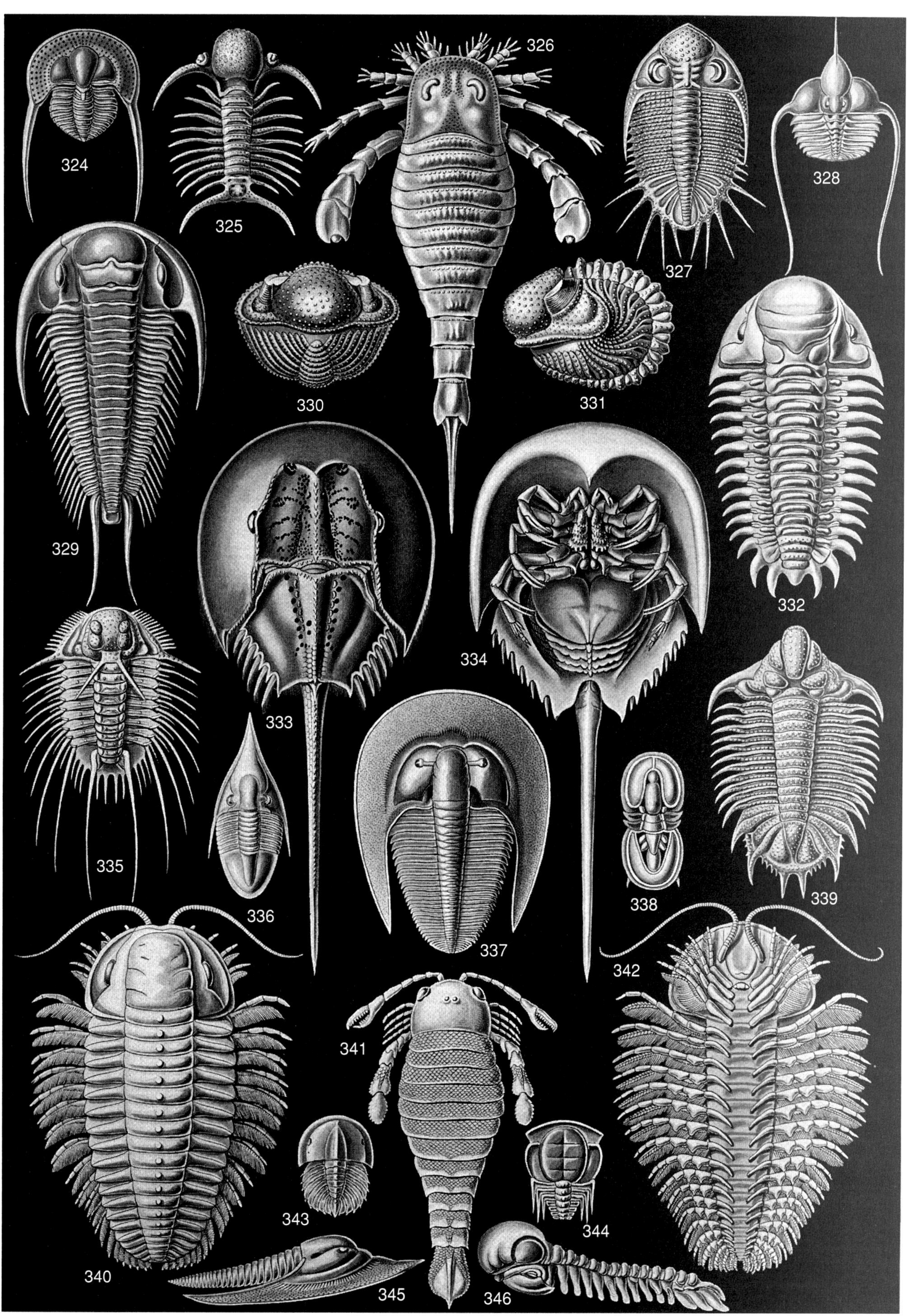


Horseshoe crabs (center) and various species of their extinct ancestors (trilobites).

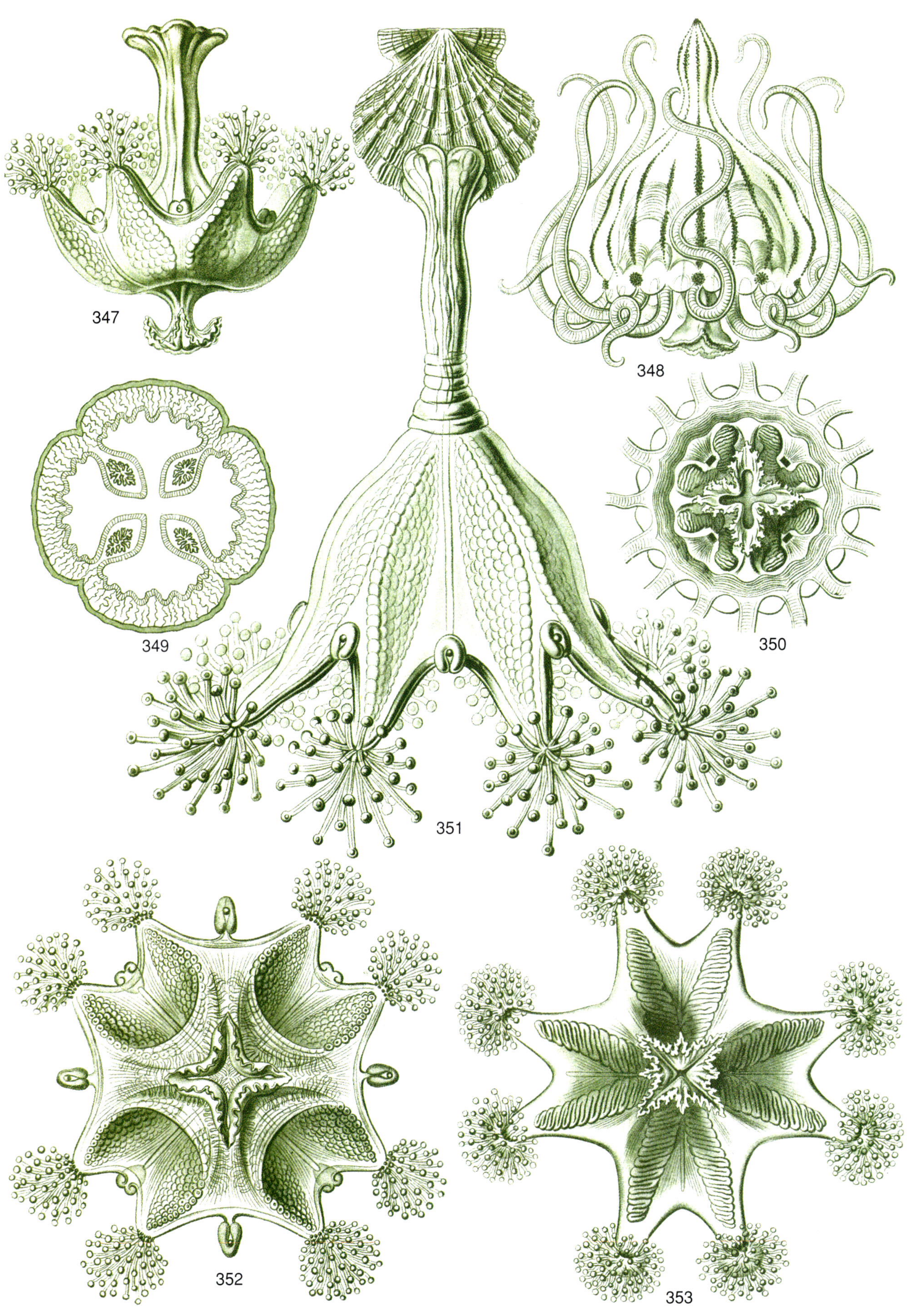


Various species of stalked jellyfishes.

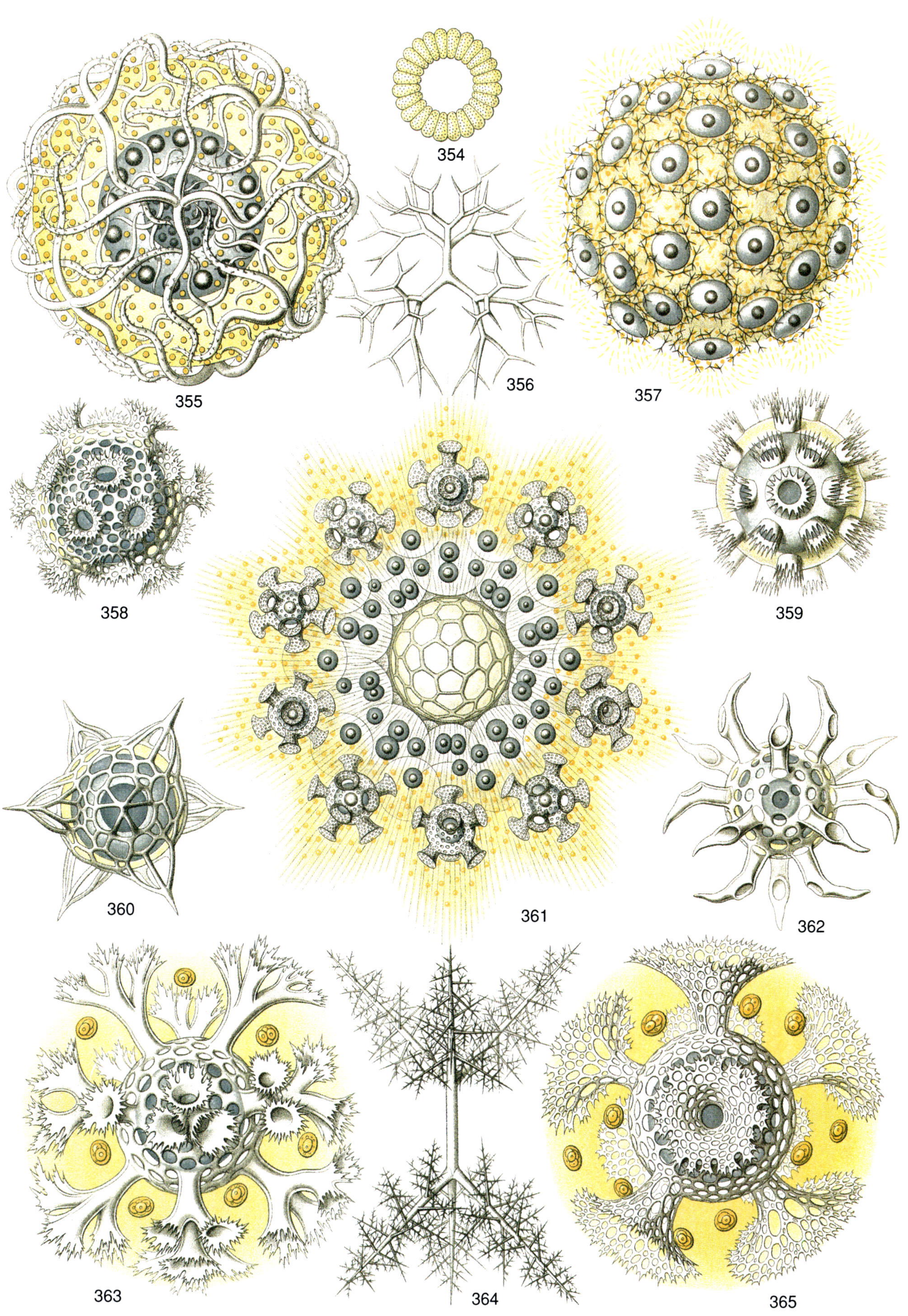


Various species of Radiolaria (a type of marine Protozoa).

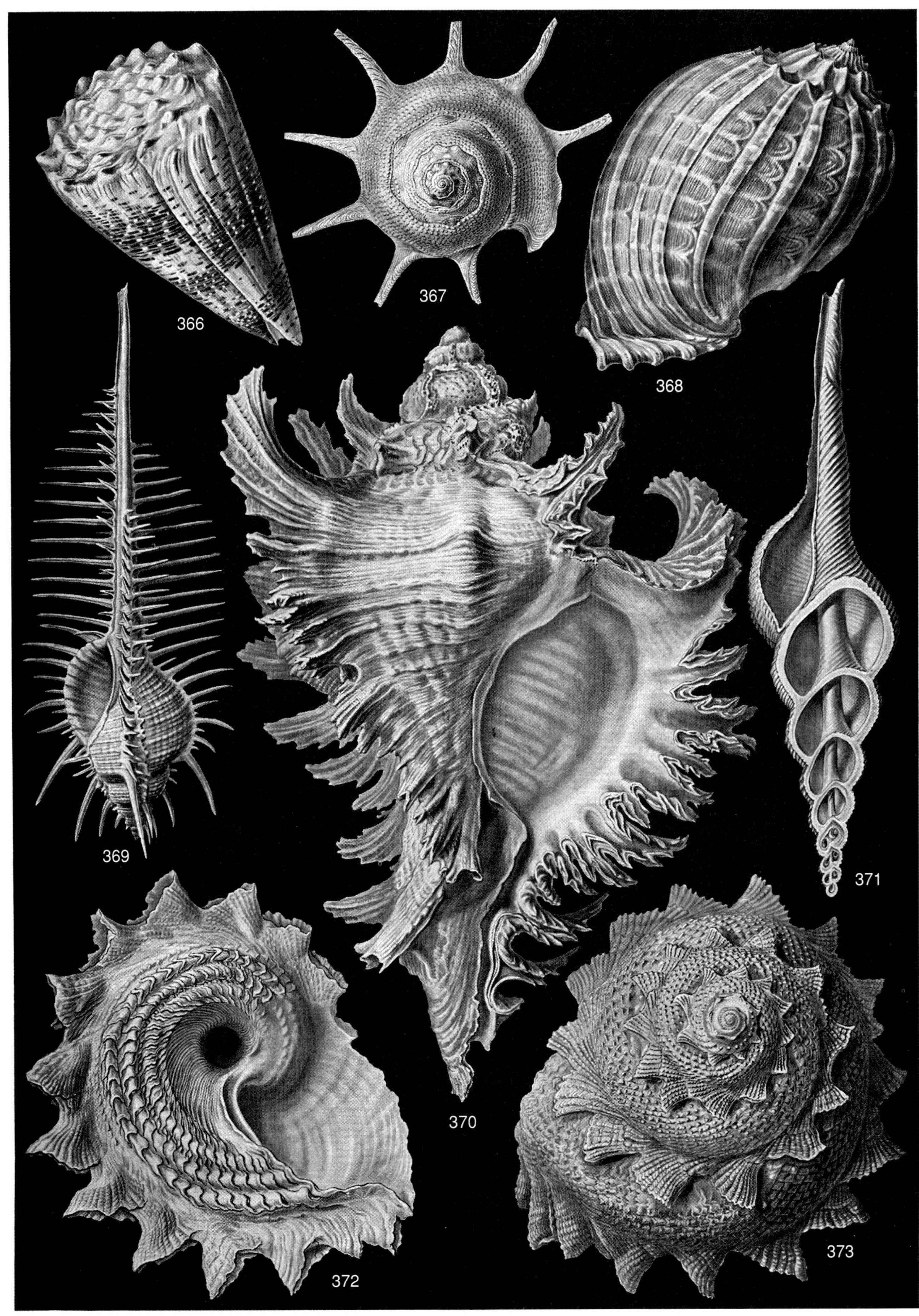




Various species of marine snails of the subclass Prosobranchia.

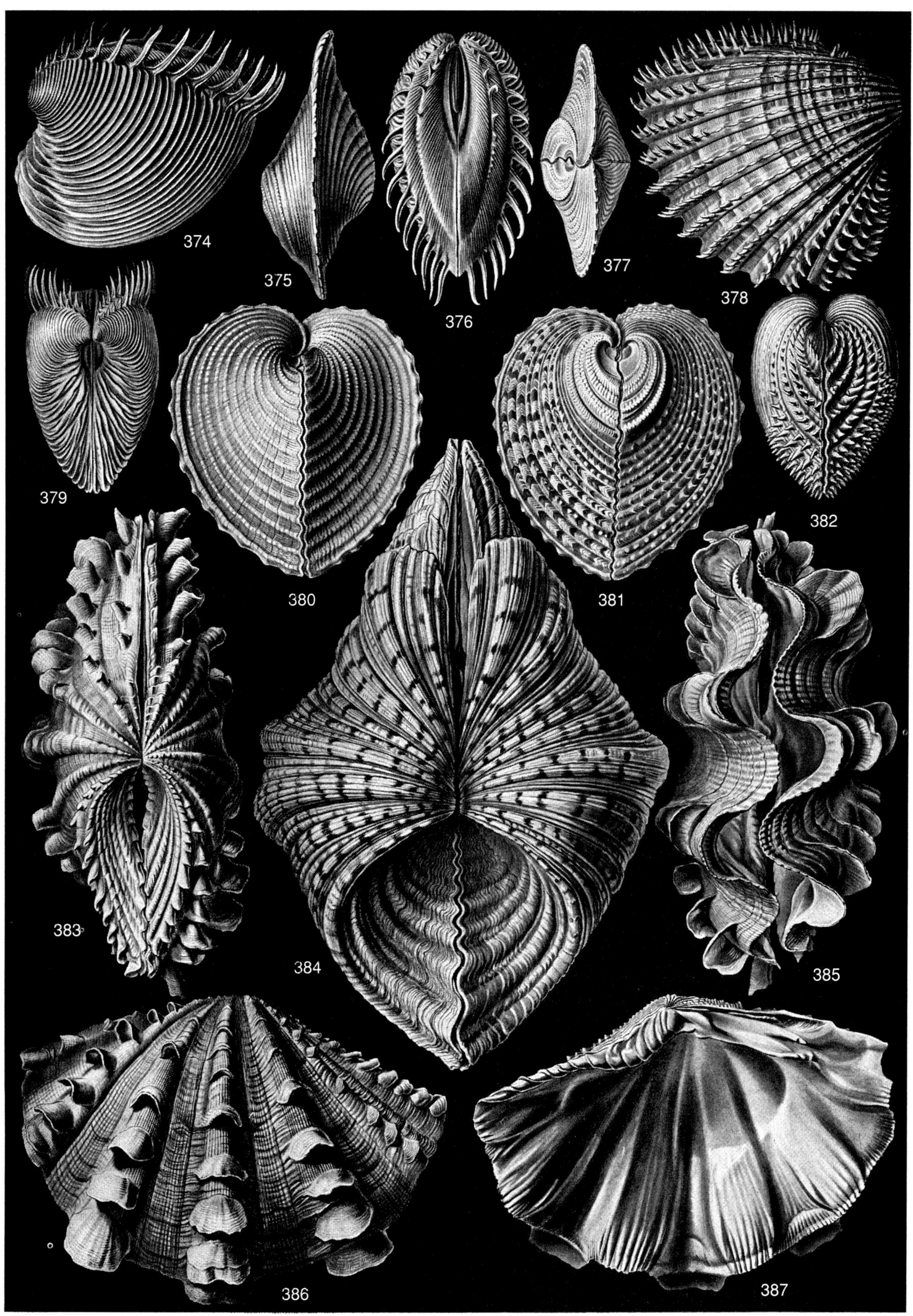


Various species of bivalves of the subclass Lamellibranchia.

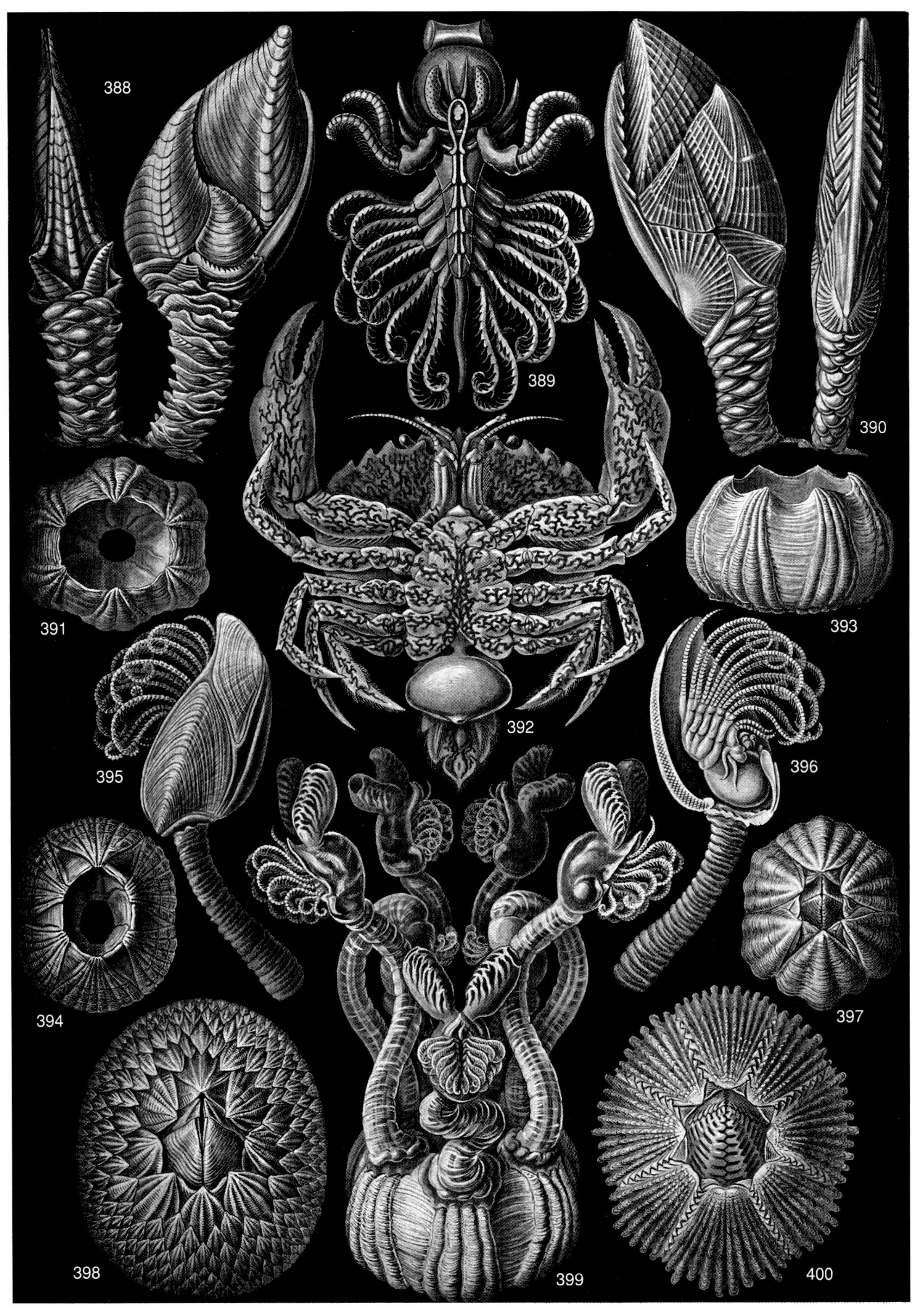




Various species of Cirripedia (barnacles and allies). The crab in the center is harboring a parasitic species of this subclass.

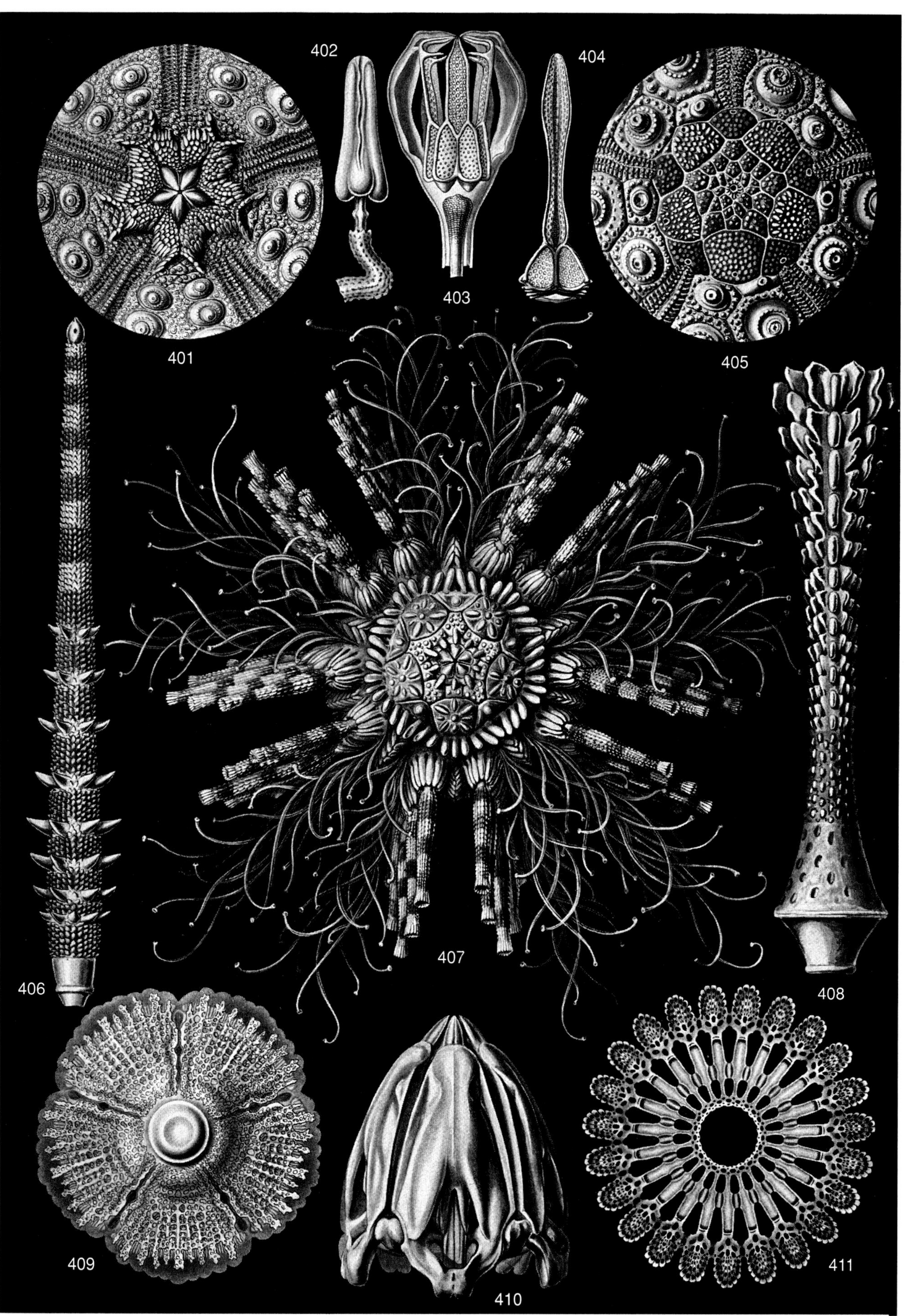


Various species of sea-urchins.

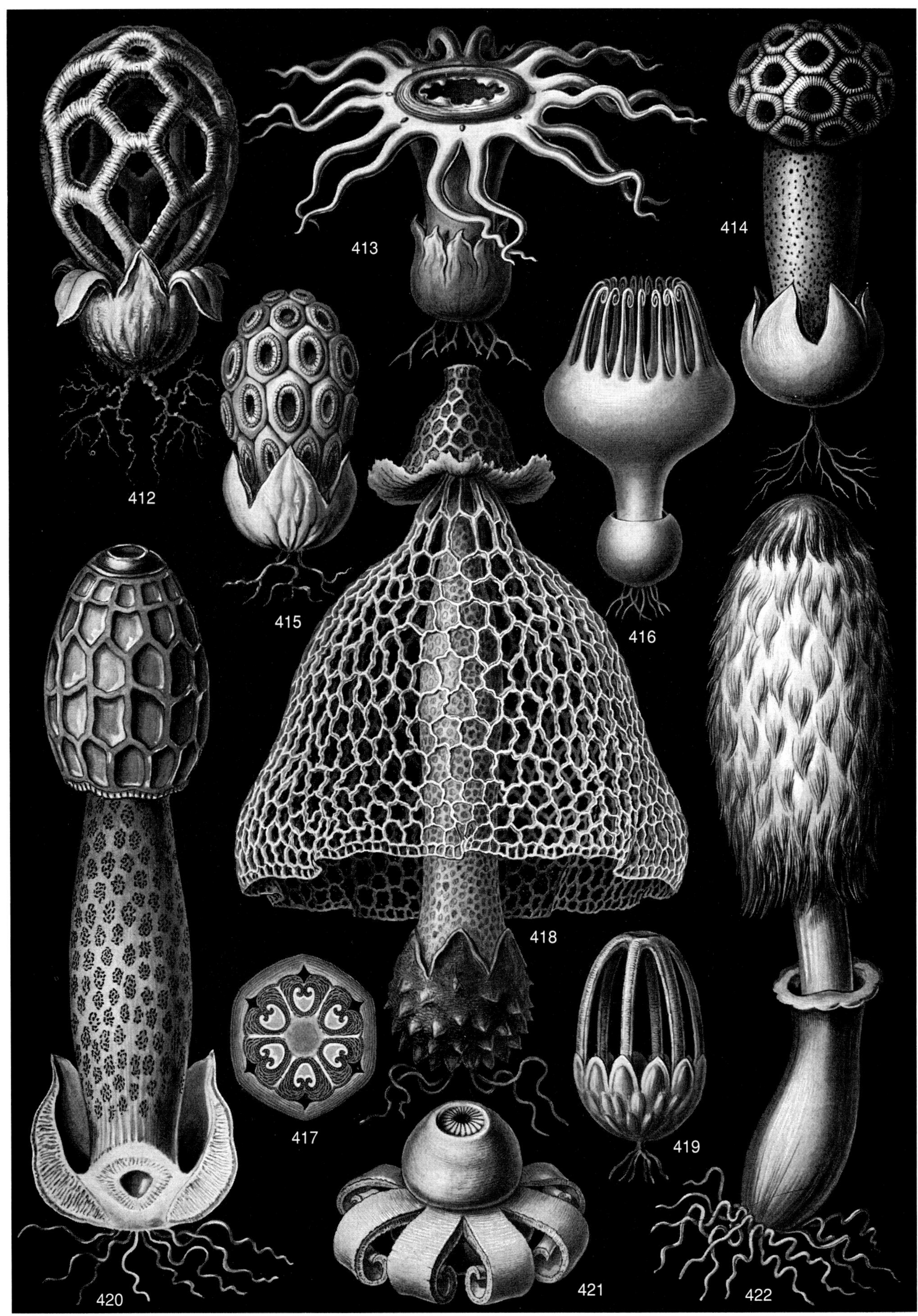


Various species of fungi of the class Basidiomycetes.

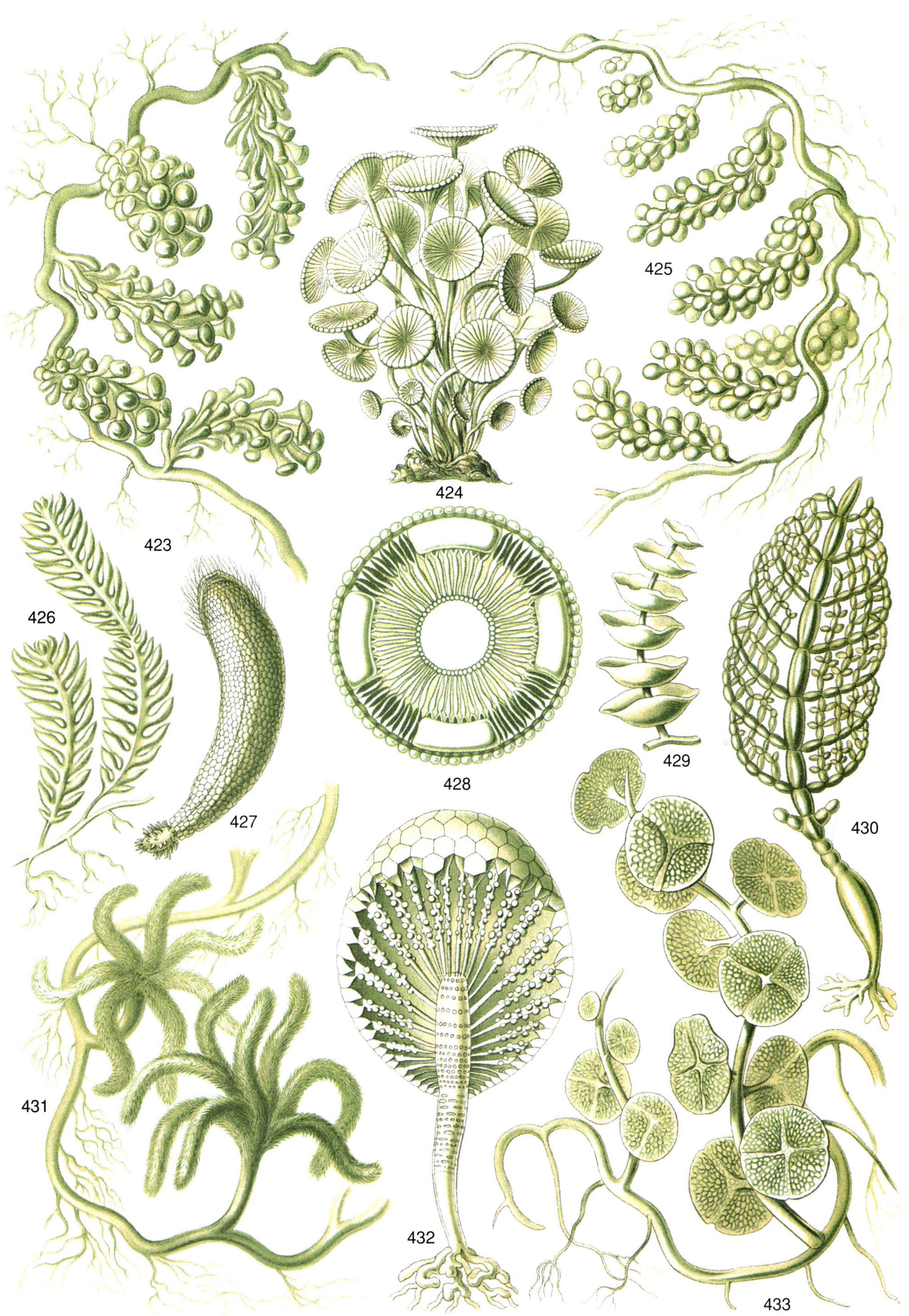


Various species of algae of the order Siphonales.

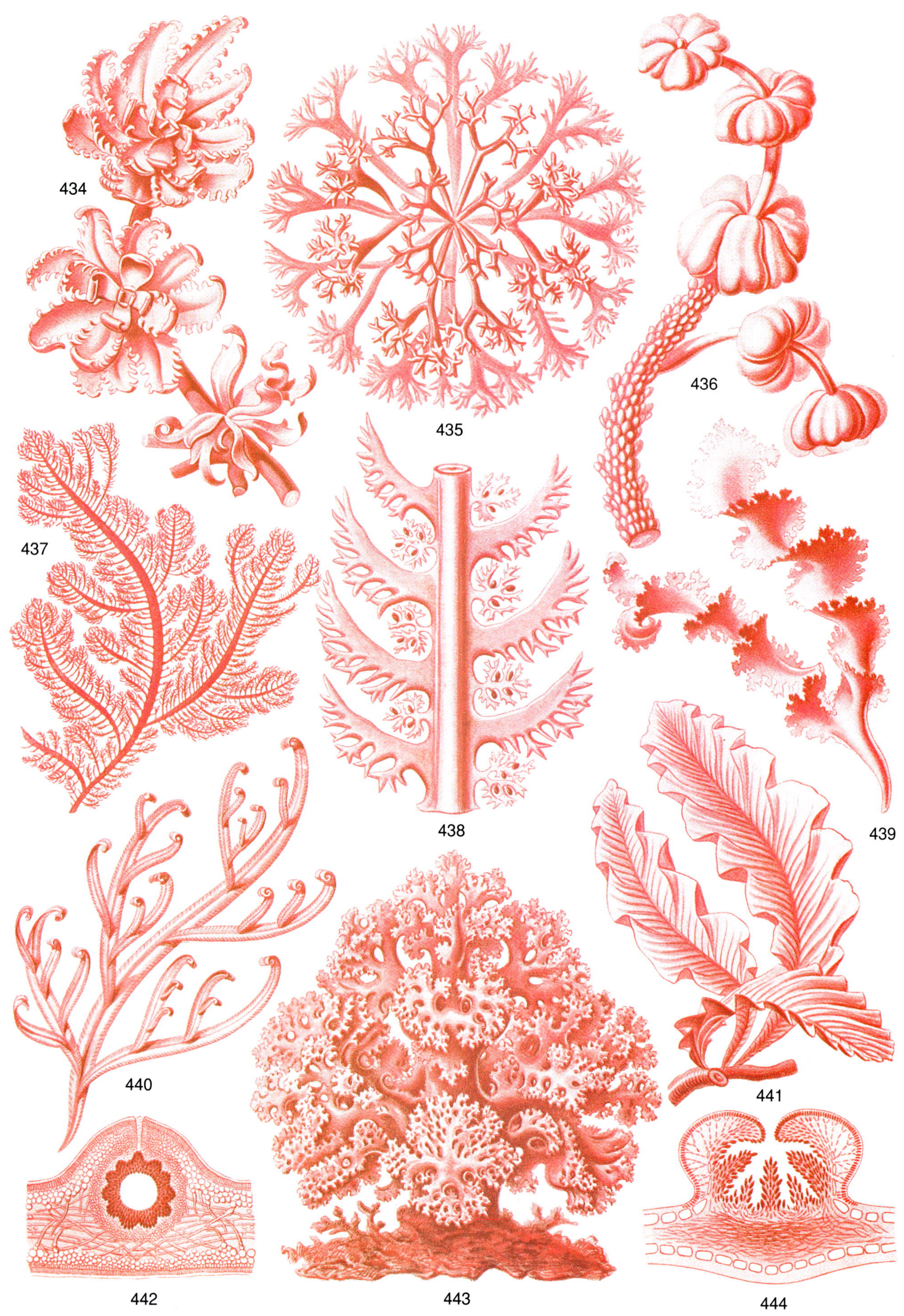




Various species of red algae (Rhodophyceae).

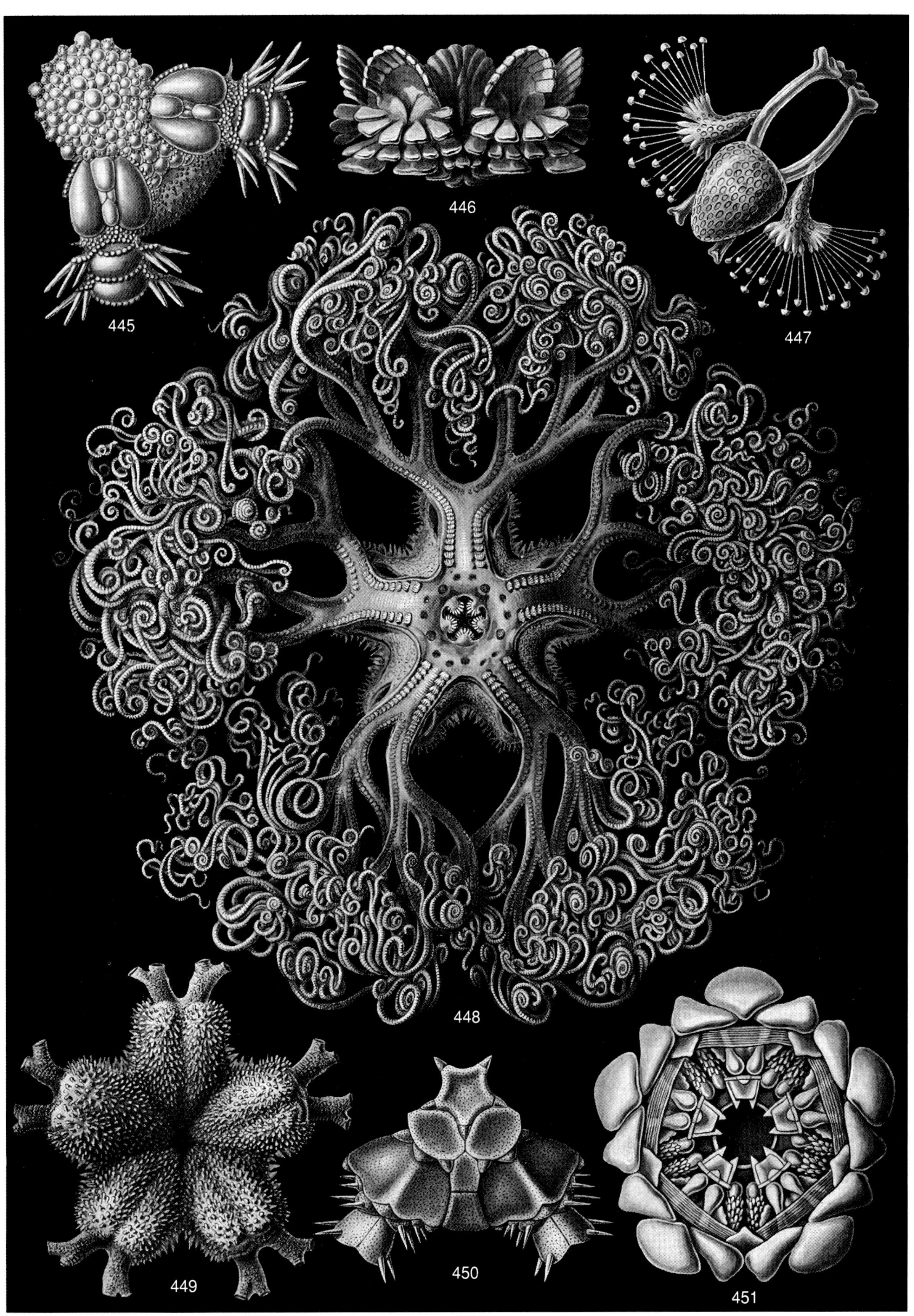


Various species of Gorgon-headed starfishes.

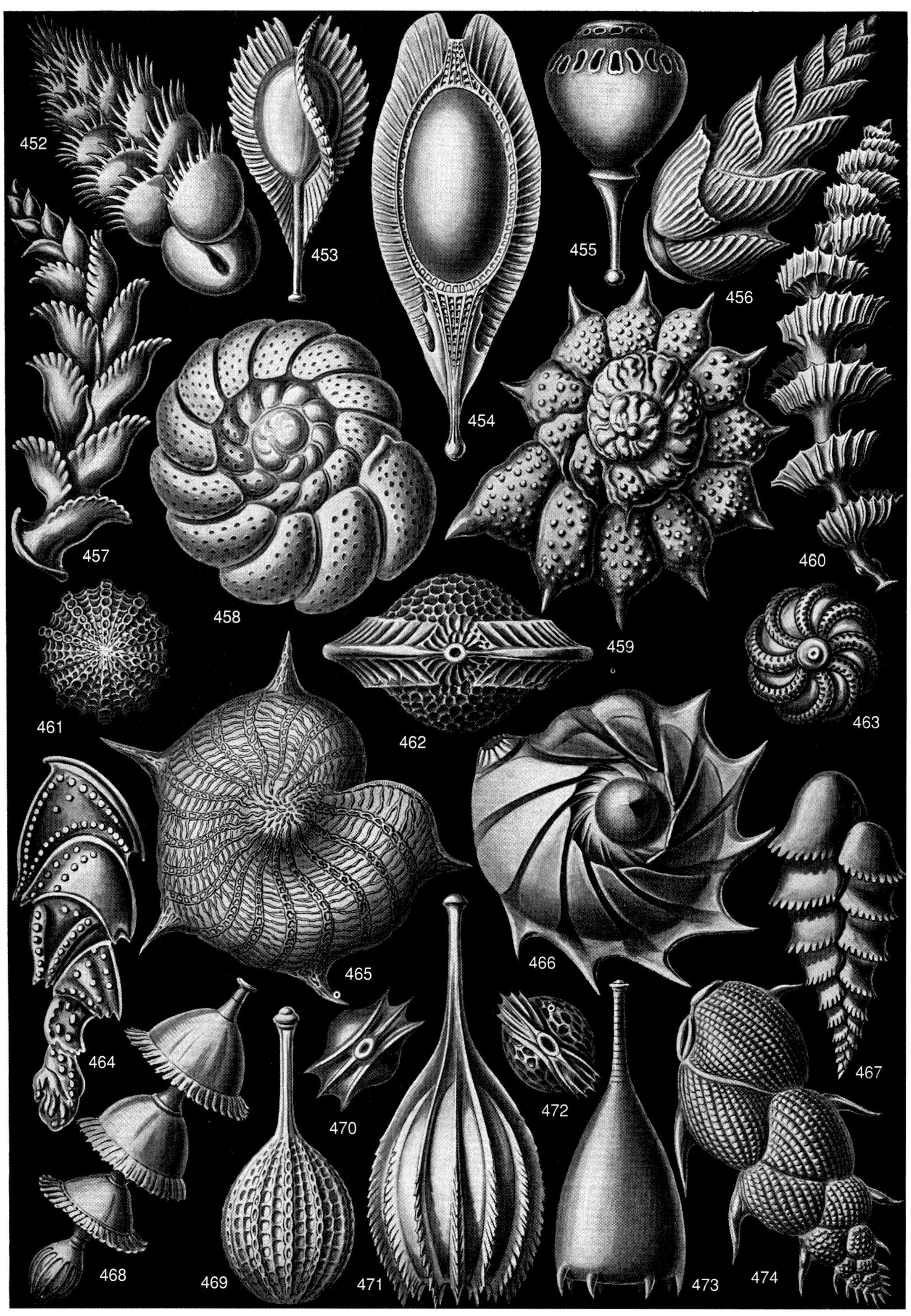


Various species of Foraminifera (a type of marine Protozoa).

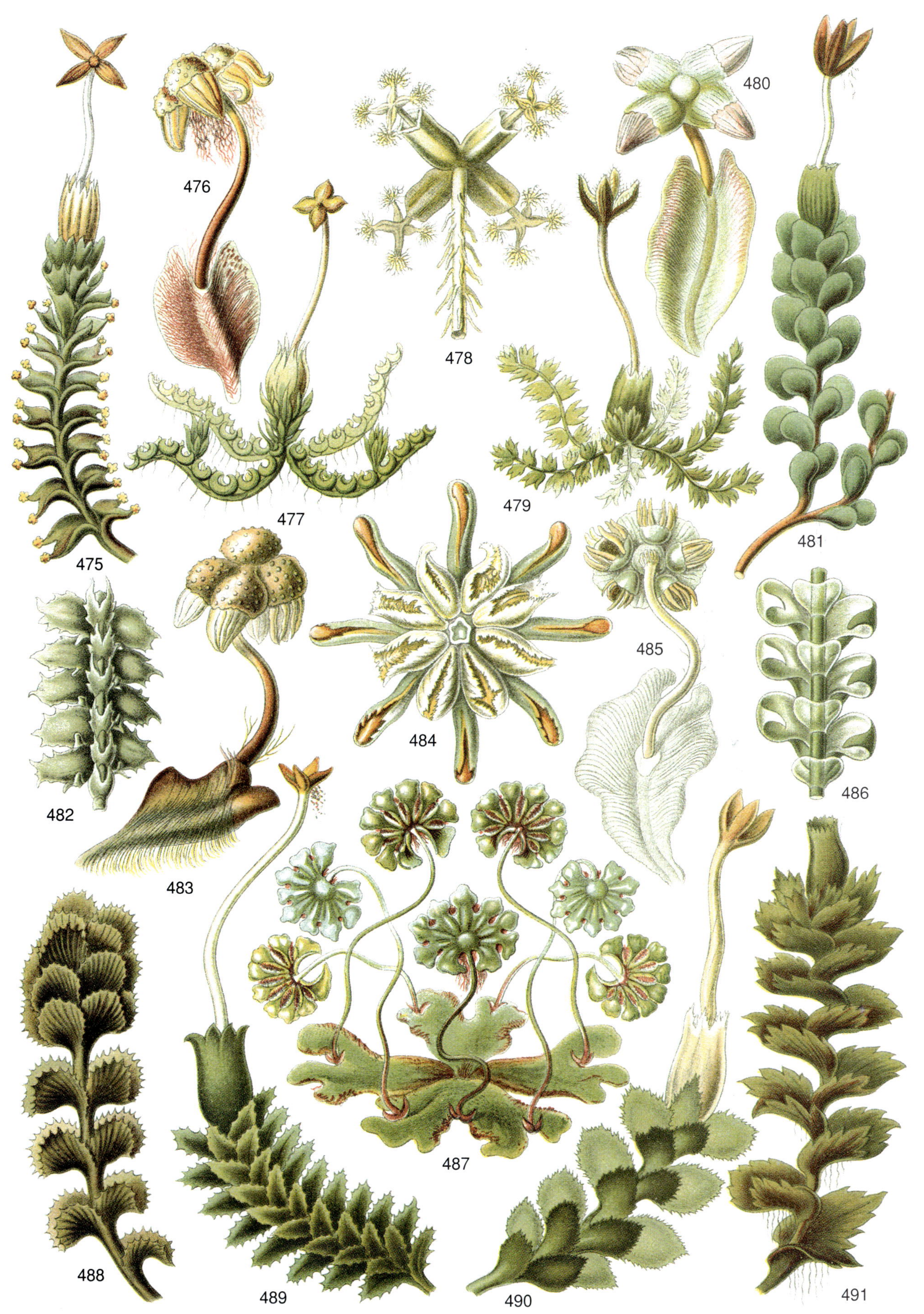


Various species of liverworts (related to mosses).

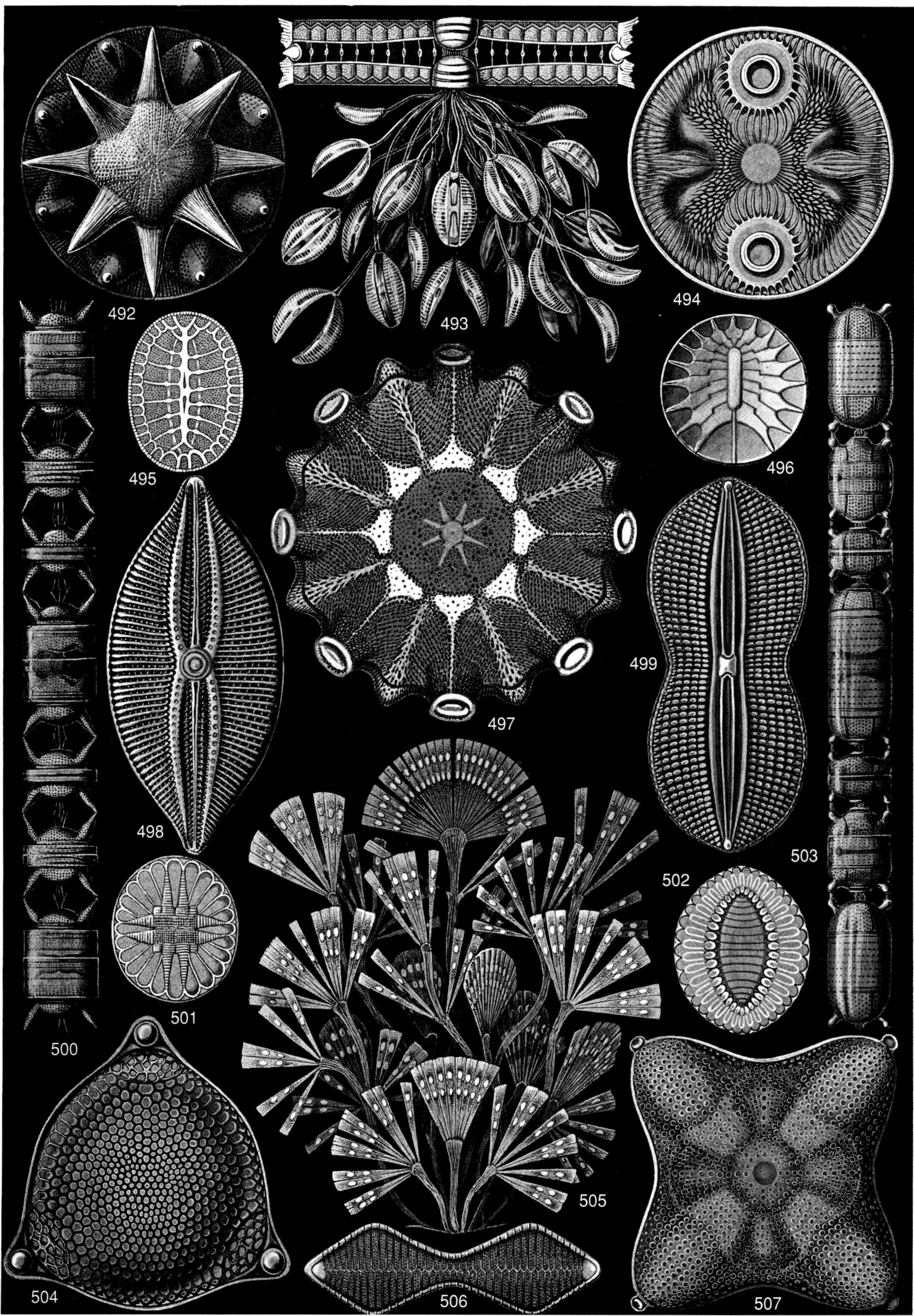




Various species of diatoms (a type of unicellular plant).

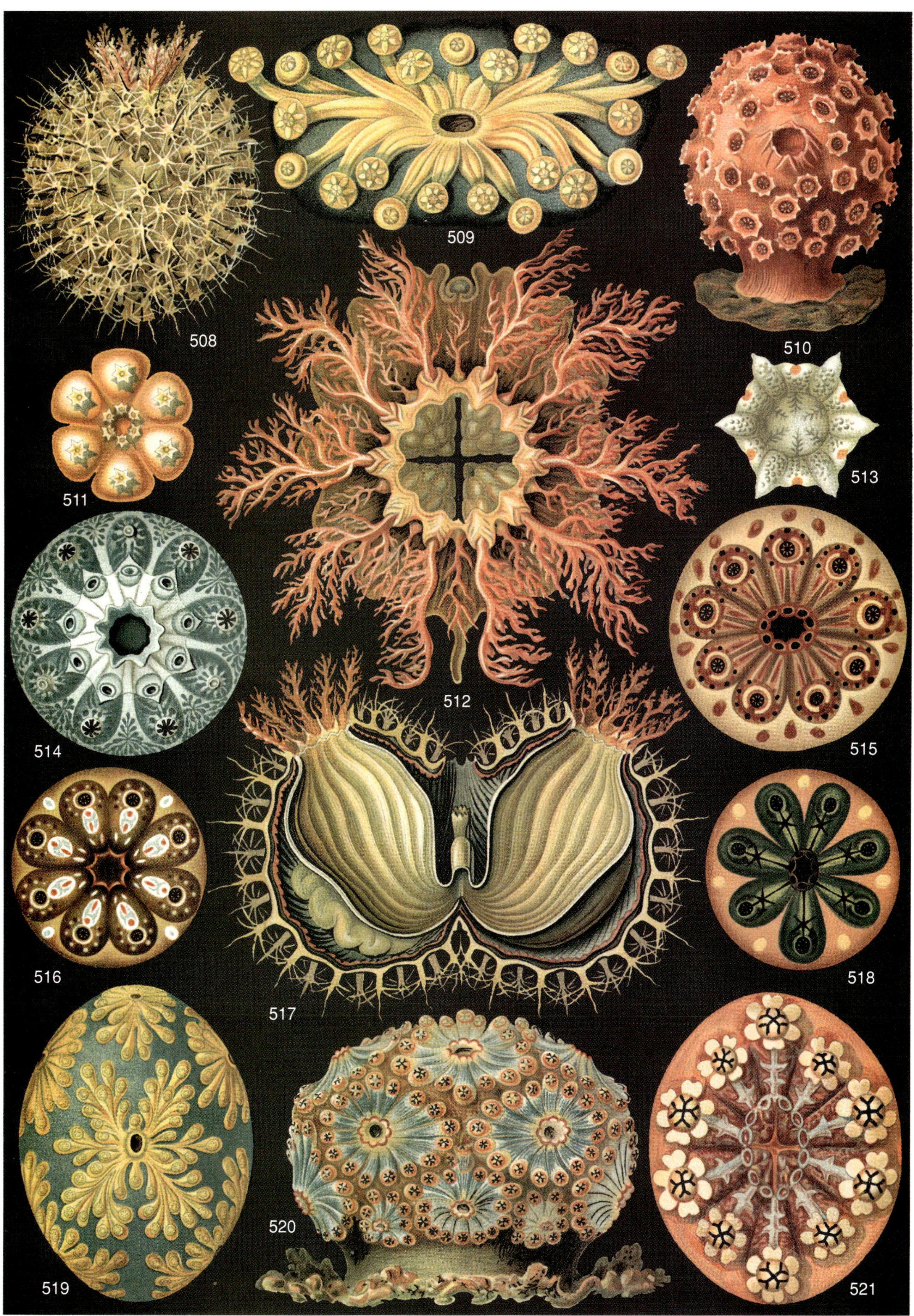


Various species of sea-squirts (a class of marine chordate animals).

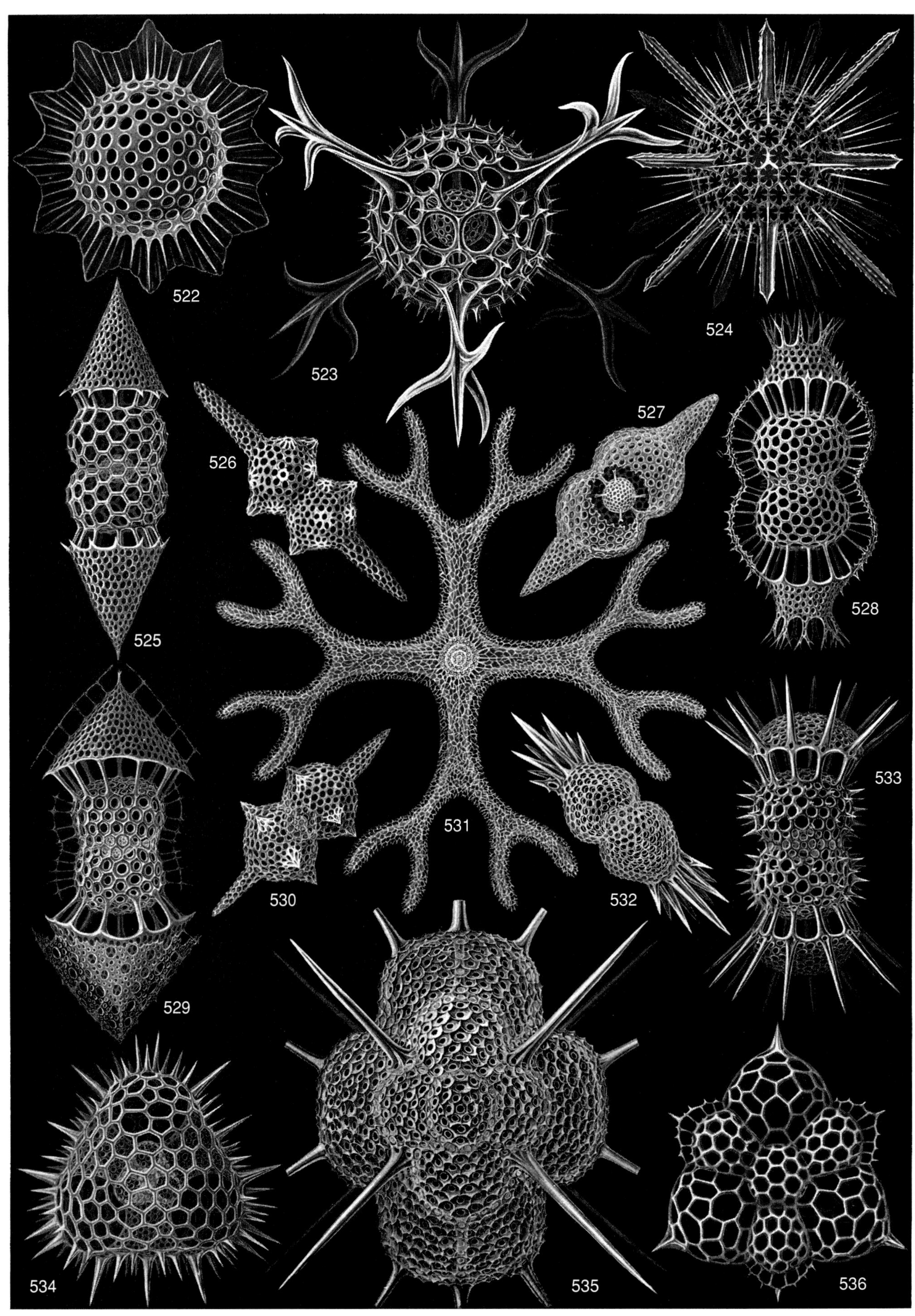




Various species of Radiolaria (a type of marine Protozoa).

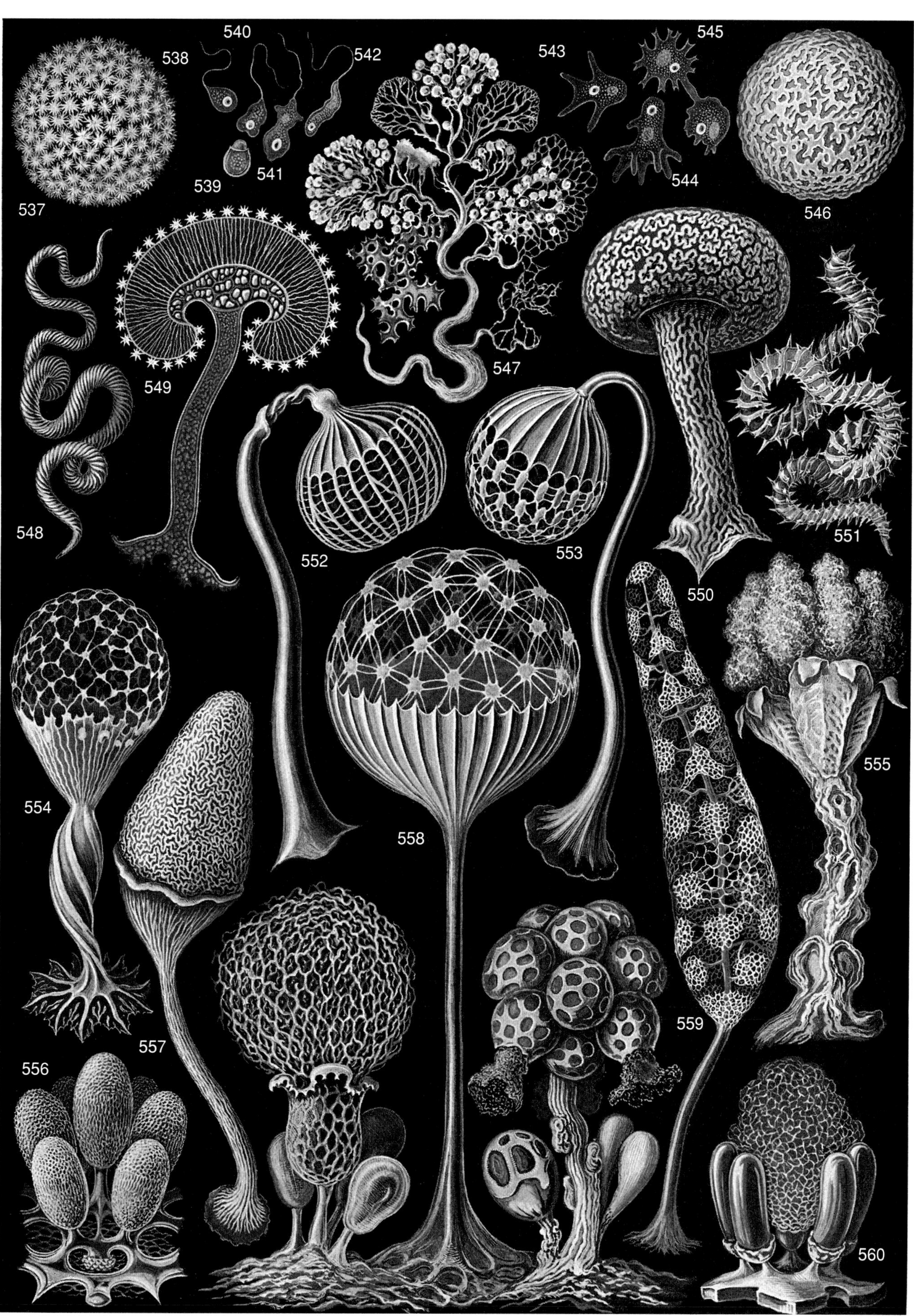


Various species of slime molds, considered by some to be plants (class Myxomycetes), by others to be animals (Mycetozoa).

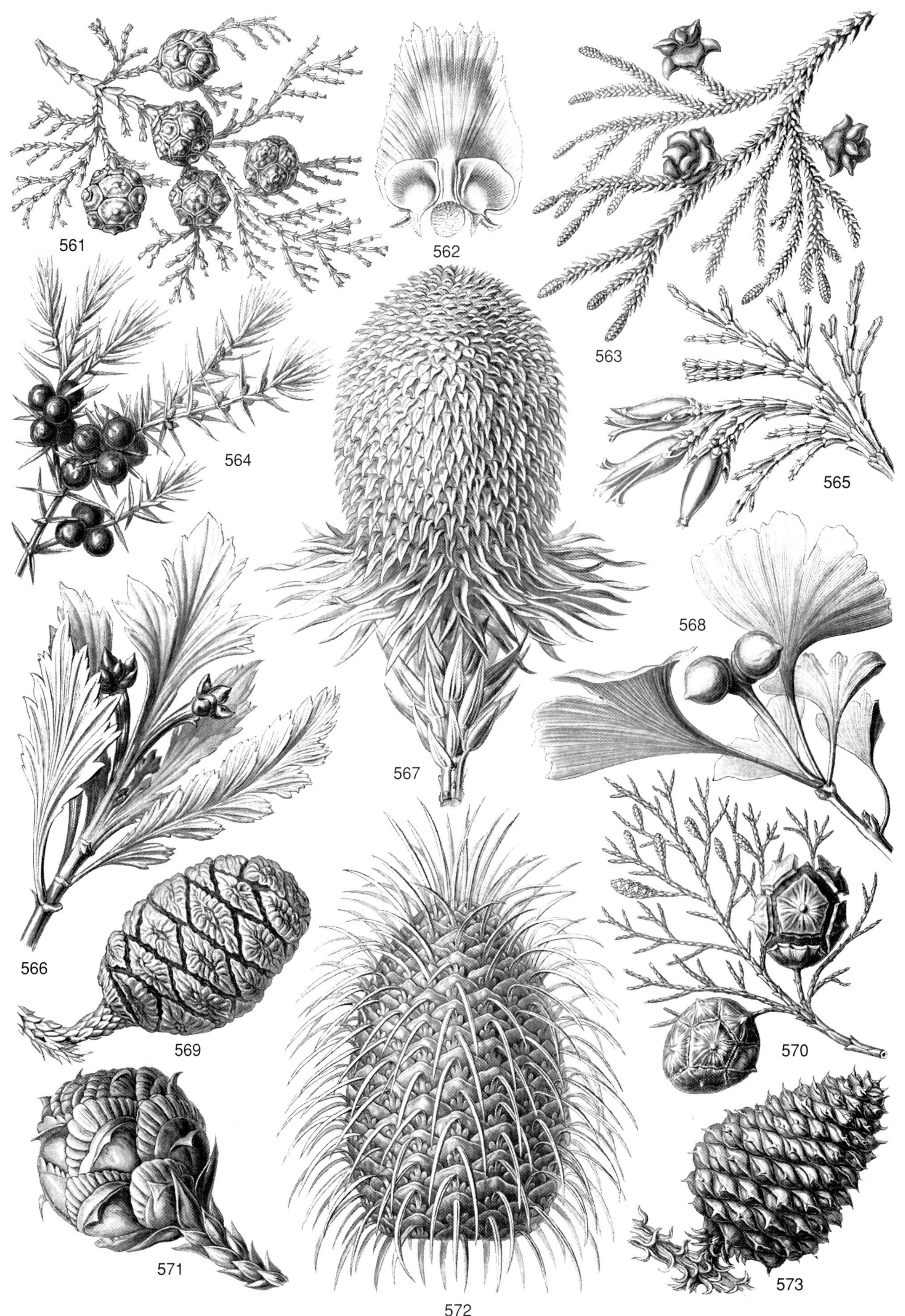




The fruit of various species of conifers.

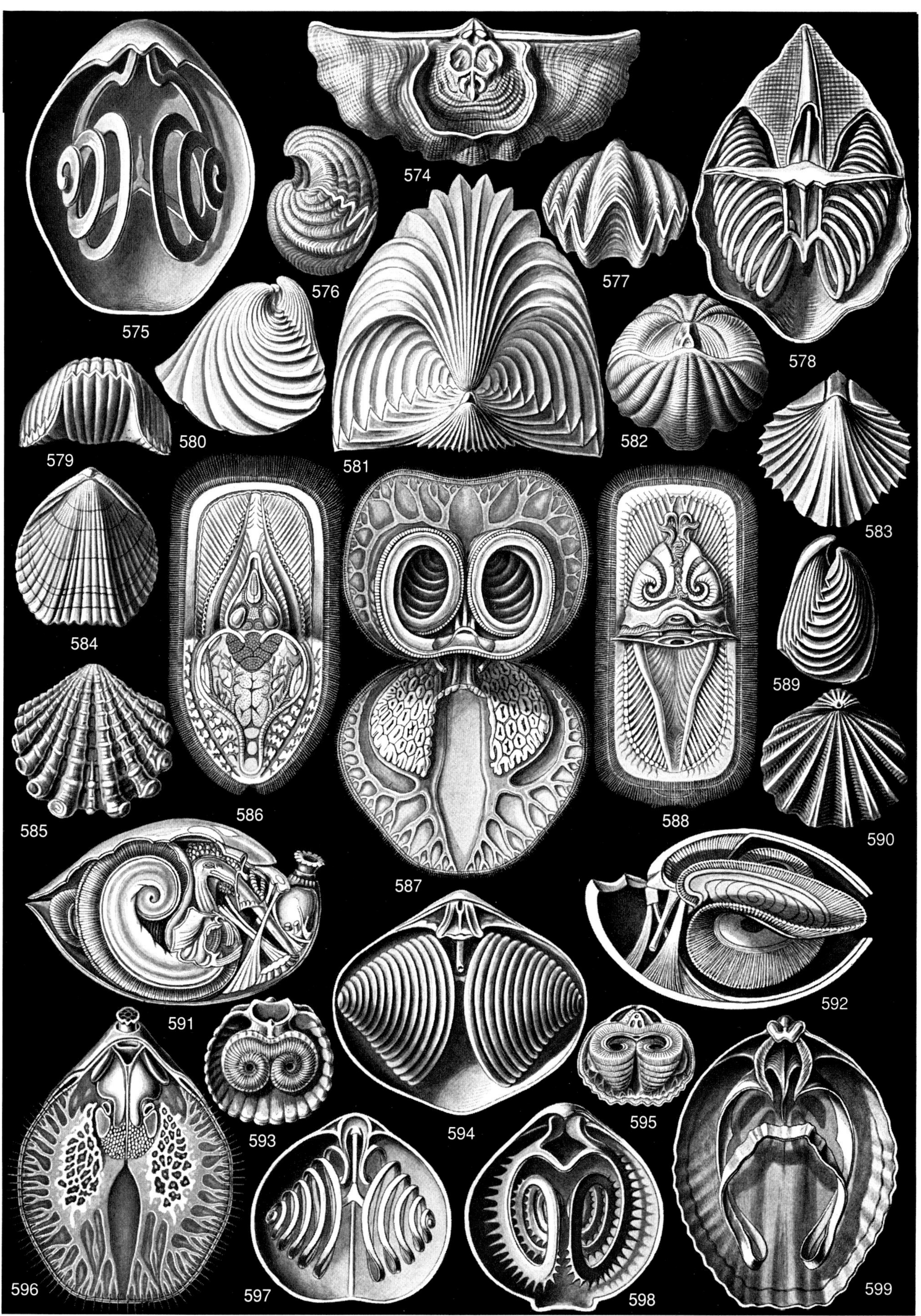


Various species of lamp-shells (phylum Brachiopoda).

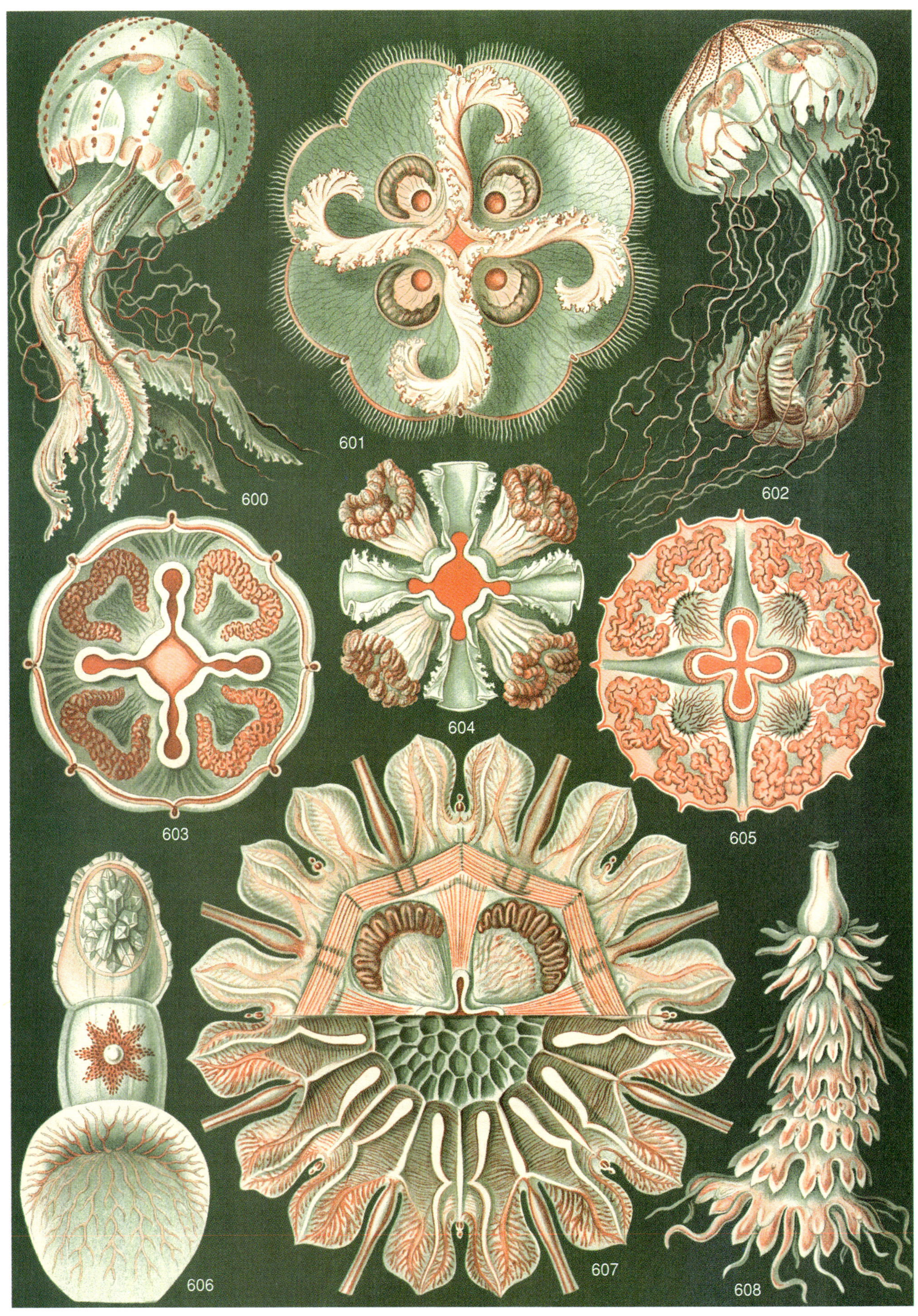


Various species of Semaeostomeae (an order of jellyfishes).